Confidence Hacks

24 Simple Habits and Techniques to Get out of Your Head and Be More Confident

David De Las Morenas
www.HowToBeast.com

Copyright © 2014 David De Las Morenas

All rights reserved.

ISBN-13: 978-1505449907
ISBN-10: 1505449901

Disclaimer

All attempts have been made to verify the information in this book; however, neither the author nor the publisher assumes any responsibility for errors, omissions, or contrary interpretations of the content within.

This book is for entertainment purposes only, and so the views of the author should not be taken as expert instruction or commands. The reader is responsible for his or her own actions.

This book is not meant to be used, nor should it be used, to diagnose or treat any medical condition. For diagnosis or treatment of any medical problem, consult your own physician. I recommend consulting a doctor to assess and/or identify any health related issues prior to making any dramatic changes to your diet and/or exercise regime.

Neither the author nor the publisher assumes any responsibility or liability on behalf of the purchaser or reader of this book.

Buyer Bonus

As a way of saying thank you for your purchase, I'm offering a FREE eBook that's exclusive to my book and blog readers.

It's called **3 Habits of Highly Effective Men** and it details a set of powerful habits and techniques men should adopt to drastically improve their confidence, charisma, discipline, and productivity.

Inside you'll learn:

• A Simple Bodyweight Routine to Build Muscle and Burn Fat

• An Easy 5 Minute Exercise to Rewire Your Brain for Confidence

• How to Approach Any Girl in Any Situation Like a Boss

Download it here: **www.HowToBeast.com/free-ebook**

Dedication

Thank you to my best friend Greg. Our endless conversations about how "confidence is everything" inspired me to write this book and share my philosophy, experience, and research on the subject thus far. Let's get it, baby.

Contents

WHO AM I TO WRITE A BOOK ABOUT CONFIDENCE? 1

WHAT EXACTLY IS CONFIDENCE? 7

THIS IS WHAT MAKES YOU CONFIDENT IN THE MOMENT 11

THIS IS WHAT MAKES YOU CONFIDENT IN YOURSELF IN THE LONG TERM 18

HOW LONG-TERM AND SHORT-TERM CONFIDENCE INTERACT WITH ONE ANOTHER AND WHAT THIS MEANS FOR YOU 25

HOW THIS BOOK WILL GIVE YOU THE SOLUTION TO BOTH SHORT-TERM AND LONG-TERM CONFIDENCE 29

1. THE SECRET TO TRANSFORMING LIMITING BELIEFS INTO EMPOWERING ONES 32

2. A SIMPLE METHOD TO LITERALLY REWIRE YOUR BRAIN TO BE MORE CONFIDENT... 37

3. A SIMPLE AFFIRMATION TO RAPIDLY DEVELOP YOUR SENSE OF SELF-WORTH 41

4. HOW TO DESIGN YOUR OWN POWERFUL AFFIRMATIONS TO BOOST SITUATIONAL CONFIDENCE 45

5. THE EASIEST WAY TO CONVEY CONFIDENCE IN ALL OF YOUR SOCIAL INTERACTIONS 49

6. THE QUICKEST WAY TO BUILD RAPPORT AND ASSUME A POSITIVE, SOCIAL MINDSET 55

7. A SHOCKING WAY TO USE YOUR OWN DEATH AS MOTIVATION TO LIVE A BOLDER, MORE CONFIDENT LIFE 59

8. HOW TO RELEASE PENT UP ANGER AND INSTANTLY ELIMINATE NEGATIVE MENTAL CHATTER 65

9. THE ONLY WAY TO FORGET SOMETHING THAT'S EATING UP YOUR CONFIDENCE FROM THE INSIDE.................................... 70

10. AN INSTANT CURE FOR TWO BIG CONFIDENCE KILLERS (SELF-LOATHING AND ANXIETY) 74

11. A SIMPLE WAY TO STOP TAKING YOURSELF SO SERIOUSLY AND STOP PLAYING THE VICTIM.. 78

12. A QUICK AT-HOME FULL-BODY WORKOUT TO IMPROVE POSTURE, STRENGTH, AND MUSCLE MASS........................... 82

13. ONE WEIRD WAY TO TRICK YOUR MIND INTO BEING MORE CONFIDENT 86

14. STAND PROUDLY: A QUICK FIX FOR POOR POSTURE 91

15. HOW TO TURN BOTH YOUR FAILURES AND SUCCESSES INTO INCREASED CONFIDENCE 96

16. HOW TO TURN OFF YOUR MIND AND SLEEP SOUNDLY EVERY SINGLE NIGHT 100

17. ONE THING EVERY MAN MUST HAVE IN ORDER TO PROJECT CONFIDENCE AND STRENGTH 102

18. HOW TO INCORPORATE FOCUS AND PURPOSE INTO YOUR DAILY LIFE... 106

19. THE SECRET TO FINDING YOUR PERFECT HAIR STYLE 109

20. HOW TO CONTROL YOUR MENTAL STATE IN TIMES OF ANXIETY AND STRESS 112

21. HOW TO SPEAK DEEPLY WITH CONFIDENCE AND AUTHORITY 115

22. A STRANGE TRICK TO SHOCK YOURSELF AND REDUCE YOUR INHIBITIONS 118

23. THE SECRET TO DRESSING SHARPLY AND APPEARING CONFIDENT 121

24. A 5 MINUTE ACTIVITY THAT WILL RELIEVE DEPRESSION AND INVIGORATE YOU 124

HOW TO COMBINE THESE HACKS AND CREATE POWERFUL, CUSTOM CONFIDENCE STACKS 128

THE BIGGEST RISK IS NOT TAKING ACTION 131

CAN YOU DO ME A FAVOR? 133

MY OTHER BOOKS 135

ABOUT THE AUTHOR 137

SCIENTIFIC REFERENCES 139

Who Am I to Write a Book about Confidence?

Throughout my life I've learned to deal with the concept of confidence on an extremely conscious and personal level. I truly believe that "confidence is everything" in the sense that your confidence level at any given moment and in regard to any given situation is the single most important factor in determining both how you perform in said activity and how you feel about yourself. And, at the end of the day, how you perform and how you feel about yourself are arguably the two most important things in life.

Like most people, I lived a carefree childhood. The carefree nature of children makes them quite comfortable in their own skin – it makes them supremely confident beings. As children, we simply haven't been socially conditioned to fear things like the disapproval of others or being the center of attention. And so we proceed without inhibitions.

However, once we enter adolescence, insecurities begin to form and we tend to become less and less confident. This happens because we tend to enter into schools with socially defined standards and norms. Students are conditioned to cherish and value the social hierarchy. If you can't be the football star, have a hot girlfriend, or have the most friends, you're often considered a failure... in your own mind, at least.

The social structure is so defined in middle school and high school that everyone, the cool and popular kid included, is self-conscious. Self-conscious in the sense that they're so aware of their appearances and actions that they incessantly worry about how they're being perceived by their peers. This prevents them from acting freely. They're so "in their heads" that they essentially construct imaginary prisons that rule their lives. The fears of being laughed at for wearing "weird" clothes or for saying something "awkward" are the prison walls that confine them.

The danger of losing your confidence at this age, or at any age for that matter, is that it can be very hard to get back. This is because it requires you to change your beliefs about yourself and your general thought patterns. Without acknowledging the issue and then pushing through the seemingly endless barriers of resistance to correct it, we often just give up and endure the mental agony that comes as a result of not feeling confident.

My adolescence was no different. My passion at the time was basketball. How I performed on the basketball court, and how I was regarded as a basketball player by my peers and coaches directly determined how happy I felt and how confident I was in other areas of my life – with girls, for example.

I was a star player all the way until high school, and so I had some insane little boy swagger. However, in my freshman year, this all changed.

I tried out and made the team, but my success essentially ended there. From the beginning of the season I felt that my coach disliked me. Whether it was true or just in my head, I played like shit and he benched me for most of the season. My confidence was crippled. I played worse and worse. And I felt terrible, too. I could barely make eye contact with other students as I walked down the hallway to my next class. The thought of even talking to girls made me tremble. I vividly remember being so anxious during a study period one day, for no apparent reason, that my hands shook uncontrollably as I tried to hold them still. I had failed at the only thing that mattered, and life sucked as a result.

That year had a profound impact on the next ten or so years of my life – a profoundly negative impact, that is. Throughout the rest of high school and even through college I failed to regain my confidence. I maintained a small social circle of friends and continued to play basketball, but I never felt fully comfortable in my own skin. I recall even feeling nervous and worthless at family gatherings, because I never had a girlfriend with me like so many of my cousins. I felt inadequate. And women, or the lack thereof, soon became another area of stress in my life.

Throughout high school, as I said, I never even talked to girls. In college this changed, but only slightly. While most of my friends were enjoying the sex-fest that is college, I didn't even lose my virginity until my third year. I hadn't had success with women in the past, and this fact stained my every thought. I was bad with girls and I was ever-aware of this fact. I thought I was ugly. And I knew I wasn't confident.

Like many people who struggle socially, I adopted introverted hobbies. Instead of going out on Friday nights and partying I would often stay in and play video games or build computers. I even became a highly skilled creator of "Counter Strike: Source" character textures using Adobe Photoshop.

I don't say all this to make fun of myself or put down people with these types of hobbies, but I can tell you from experience that not balancing them with socially extroverted ones that involve other people, particularly of the opposing gender, is not healthy. Humans are social creatures by nature and denying this fact is setting yourself up for depression.

And to re-iterate: my lack of confidence is what led me down the path I detailed above. I didn't think I was worthy of attracting women, being a good basketball player, or feeling awesome about myself… and so I didn't.

Fast forward until now, roughly three years after college, and I'm a completely different person. I'm not a professional basketball player, no, but I've come a long way. I've published a handful of books. I've started my own company. I've quit a corporate job to pursue a side career in personal training because of a passion I developed for fitness. I've dated more women than I can count and been in a couple of amazing long term relationships. I've even coached hundreds of men to help them improve their health and confidence.

But most importantly, I now wake up nearly every day feeling confident. I feel more-than-comfortable in my own skin as I go through my day, and I feel like I'm truly living the life that was meant for me. I can walk down the street with my head up. I can look you straight in the eye and give you a firm handshake. I can walk into a job interview and have the interviewer feel like she's the one on the spot. I can approach a cute girl without hesitating whenever I notice one that strikes me.

I've developed a strong sense of confidence. And I've done it with a focused eye and attention to detail regarding the process that got me here. This is not to say that "I've made it" or "I'm the shit." In fact, the more I grow and accomplish, the more I realize I don't know that much about so many things, and the more I feel detached from my ego. This introduction is only meant to impress upon you the distinct difference between where I am now and where I was for the greater part of my life.

I firmly believe I can use the skills I've developed as a personal coach and bestselling author to offer you valuable reference material for boosting your confidence. I'll do this by providing you with an invaluable set of hobbies, habits, activities, and lifestyle changes that will assist you in this mission. These are some of the most effective things that I used to develop this confidence, and I've seen other people use them to achieve similarly powerful results. Most of them I still use quite often, especially when I find myself in a down, depressed, or anxious mood. They're all designed to get you out of your head, stop you from overthinking things, and instead get you living life and going after what you want.

What Exactly Is Confidence?

We all know that confidence is a good thing. Having a high degree of self-confidence leads to symptoms like feeling better about yourself, performing better at any given activity, and possessing better social skills. And these qualities, in turn, generally lead to things like better jobs, more money, hotter women, more sex, and more fulfilling friendships, just to name a few.

Before continuing, I believe it's invaluable for us to pause for a moment and reconsider our preexisting notions of confidence, as well as what exactly the word means.

I have to assume you're reading this book because you feel that you're lacking confidence. Honestly, we could all use a confidence boost. But here's the thing: we usually don't stop and define exactly what this magical word—confidence—means.

I think once you examine what confidence really is on a conscious level that your confidence, and even more so your ability to build confidence, will drastically improve. This is precisely why I'm including this chapter.

The dictionary defines confidence as follows: *noun, belief in oneself and one's powers or abilities.*

And that's exactly what confidence is: a **belief** – more specifically a belief in yourself and your abilities. When you're feeling confident, you believe that you can handle a particular situation as you'd like to. When you're not feeling confident, you don't possess this belief. Instead you're unsure of your ability to handle a situation, or even doubtful of it. And this makes you feel anxious and usually cripples your performance.

The implications of this fact (that confidence is simply a belief) are profound. This is because beliefs are extremely potent things. We don't have to look any further than the existence of placebo effects to see why this is true.

For those of you who are unaware, a placebo is a simulated or otherwise medically ineffectual treatment for a disease or medical condition, the intention of which is to deceive the patient, who fully believes they're receiving proper treatment. Basically, a placebo treatment is using a fake drug or procedure (one that has no real effects – think of a sugar pill with no active ingredients or a "for show" surgery) on a patient that's truly sick, often in hopes of actually curing them.

The astounding thing about placebo treatments is that they actually work a large percentage of the time. This medical phenomenon is being studied more and more by contemporary scientific researchers. A number of real physiological responses have been measured, from changes in heart rate and blood pressure to chemical activity in the brain. And they've been measured in a wide variety of situations, from cases involving pain, depression, anxiety, and fatigue to even being used successfully for some symptoms of Parkinson's disease (1).

People's bodies are essentially altering and curing themselves. And the only possible explanation for these borderline miraculous results is that the belief that they've been administered effective treatments stimulates unconscious healing processes in their bodies. These patients **believe** that they've been given medicine or surgeries that will fix them, and that's been enough for their brains and bodies to take care of the rest. It's truly amazing.

So when I say *beliefs are extremely powerful*, this is what I mean. If our minds are powerful enough to make actual physiological changes to our bodies when the correct beliefs are present, then the notion that self-confidence can drastically change how we look, feel, and perform should seem obvious.

What I want you to take from this chapter is the following:

1. Confidence is belief in yourself and your abilities – it starts and ends in your head. There is nothing specific you need to achieve or prove to someone else to become confident. There is no amount of time you need to wait before you can build confidence. The only person who can get in your way is you.

2. Beliefs have been proven powerful enough to cause our bodies to alter themselves and even cure diseases. By changing your beliefs about yourself and your abilities, you will in turn experience real, measurable changes in everything from your mood and energy to your actual performance in specific activities.

Before we get to the specific recommended habits, activities, and changes that make up the meat of this book, I want to explore what I believe to be the two distinct types of confidence that you must master in order to develop unbreakable self-assurance:

1. Confidence in yourself and your abilities in the moment.

2. Confidence in yourself and your identity in the long term.

This Is What Makes You Confident in the Moment

When people talk about confidence, they're usually referring to this type. This is the confidence that someone demonstrates in the moment. It's the confidence that allows you to calmly walk into a job interview and answer challenging questions without feeling an ounce of stress. It's the confidence that allows you to coolly approach a cute girl and flirt with her before asking for her phone number. It's the confidence that allows you to take the game winning shot without trembling or shaking nervously.

The question is: what allows someone to be able to do the above things – what makes someone confident in the moment? One seemingly obvious answer is repetition – doing something over and over again tends to lead to a certain level of confidence and self-assuredness in regard to that particular activity. Approaching women, for example, is something that makes most men's knees shake. However, if you're able to push past the initial resistance against approaching a girl in public, and you're able to do it several hundred times, you're likely to become quite confident and comfortable doing so.

While repetition is definitely part of it, there's more

here than meets the eye. Some skills, like shooting a basketball or drawing a painting, require more than just confidence. They require learned skills and motor patterns. For example, even if I were put in front of a canvas and given a variety of paint brushes, and then drugged with some confidence-inducing compounds, I still wouldn't produce much more than some basic shapes and colors. Yes, my attempt would likely be better than if I were being watched by a crowd of thousands of people and had a gun to my head, because my confidence would likely suffer in that scenario. But I still wouldn't possess the raw skill needed to produce a real piece of art.

The same goes for basketball. I've played basketball my whole life. And so I possess a relatively high degree of skill. However, my confidence level has been more than a little volatile throughout my career. As I said in the introductory chapter, in high school my confidence suffered greatly. This resulted in my on court performance suffering as well. My actual skill level didn't change overnight, but my confidence sure did.

So while confidence plays a large role in all activities, it accounts for a far greater percentage of your overall performance in non-skill activities, like approaching women or being interviewed for a job. This is because these are areas where you're generally fully capable of performing at a high level – you know what to do and you can physically do it –

yet the stressful nature of them can easily cripple your performance in the moment. And therefore confidence is the main variable in your success at the end of the day. Confidence is what gets you the girl. Confidence is what gets you the job.

As a side note, I do believe there are some learned skills that go into approaching women and interviewing, but the fact is that most guys know more or less what they should say and how they should act in these types of situations, yet they struggle to actually do so because of poor confidence.

The fact is that repetition improves your confidence in these activities just the same as for skill activities, where you may actually be improving your craft as you go. This is because repetition slowly removes the self-doubt and negative self-talk that can sabotage your efforts.

Every time that you complete a particular activity you **worry** a little bit less. You stop telling yourself that you can't do something, because you've proven to yourself that you can. You stop anticipating a poor result, because you've seen positive ones. And this is essentially what confidence stems from in the moment: *the lack of negative self-talk*.

It's not that you're telling yourself how good you are at something or that you know you're the best; it's simply that you're not sabotaging your performance with doubt and anxiety. So, at the end of the day, what makes you confident in the short term is being able to turn off your mind and let the subconscious parts of your nervous system take control of your body. And the great thing is that certain techniques exist to assist you in reaching a confident, anxiety-free mental state – techniques other than endless hours of repetition. And this is one reason I'm writing this book.

The practices and activities I'll share with you are meant to target the underlying stressors and tensions that manifest themselves as internal conflict, doubt, and negative self-talk in your everyday life. By alleviating and releasing these internal triggers, you put yourself in a far better place to live life without all the negative bullshit that can creep up on you and cripple your confidence in the moment.

Before continuing I'd like to share with you some research that falls in line with my ideas. You may have heard of Mihaly Csikszentmihalyi and his experiments on *flow*. If you haven't, I'll give you a brief rundown.

After becoming impressed with artists who had the ability to lose themselves in their work, Csikszentmihalyi became intrigued. He watched them as they worked for hours, or even days straight while disregarding their needs for things like food, water, and even sleep. His obsession with this phenomenon led him to conduct research and experiments on a wide variety of individuals, from dominant athletes to fearless businessmen.

His conclusion was that there exists a state of pure immersion that we can all experience. This state is marked by full involvement, complete focus, and enjoyment of the process or activity at hand. It's when you're completely absorbed in what you're doing to the point that your mind is basically switched off. You've probably experienced it at some point while playing a sport, writing a paper, playing a video game, playing a musical instrument, or doing something similar. You're in the zone, and things like time, other people, and other items on your schedule don't even seem to exist.

This theory ties into the above definition of short-term confidence because to enter into a flow state you clearly must be able to proceed without being held back by any form of anxiety or self-doubt.

The question, of course, is has the research into this area uncovered any magical way to get into a flow state that we can use as a shortcut to confidence? The answer is not quite, but in 2013, one researcher, Owen Schaffer, proposed the following seven conditions for getting into flow. They shine some light on this question.

1. Knowing what to do

2. Knowing how to do it

3. Knowing how well you are doing

4. Knowing where to go (if navigation is involved)

5. High perceived challenges

6. High perceived skills

7. Freedom from distractions

Items 1-6 are all skill related conditions, so I won't delve deeply into those. They basically state that you need to be doing something that you know how to do, at a level that's challenging, but not too challenging. And this makes sense: to be able to confidently complete a given task, you've got to know what the hell you're doing and it needs to be enticing enough that you're not completely bored.

Number 7 is the item of interest to us because it doesn't relate to a specific skill, but rather is applicable to confidence across the board. It tells us that the main limitation to getting into flow is distraction. This is the kicker. If you can't turn your mind off and avoid distractions then you cannot enter a fully confident and immersed state. And the fact is that distractions usually stem from doubts and anxieties, whether they're linked to what you're doing, how you feel about yourself, or something else going on in your life.

I offer you this tangent on flow to solidify my claim that confidence in the moment is all about turning your mind off and removing negative thoughts and anticipations. And this is exactly what the hacks I'll offer you are meant to accomplish.

This Is What Makes You Confident in Yourself in the Long Term

Long-term confidence is a completely different beast than short-term confidence. They're both marked by a belief in yourself and your abilities. But short-term confidence manifests itself as a lack of negative self-talk in regard to specific activities in the moment. Long-term confidence, on the other hand, manifests itself through the presence of an all-around healthy self-image that's built over time.

We all have values that have grown and developed inside of us over time. They've been shaped collectively by all of our experiences. Our friends, family members, mentors, and even enemies have done their part and contributed to our ideas of what we believe and what we value.

So, before I continue, I want you to answer the following question: *what exactly do you value? What types of traits, characteristics, tendencies, etc. do you strive to possess? What type of men do you respect? What type of man do you strive to be?*

Your answer could be literally anything. Mine would include some of the following things:

- Independence and self-reliance – the ability to live and be happy completely on my own.

- Entrepreneurship – making a living by creating value on my own instead of helping someone else achieve their dream.

- Physical strength – growing and cultivating my body to embody the same strength that I strive for mentally.

- Courage – the ability to pursue what I want and act how I'd like regardless of pressure or resistance that would have me do otherwise.

- Self-discipline – the ability to do the things that I need to do despite laziness, and to avoid the things I know I shouldn't do despite temptation.

Write down a brief list of things that you value right now. We'll come back to this in a moment.

The reason I ask you to identify your values is because they're at the heart of long-term confidence. Without knowing what your values are it's nearly impossible to possess the strength of character that's necessary for long-term confidence. That's because long-term confidence is derived from the knowledge that you're living in line with your values.

When what you do on a daily basis aligns with your core values, you'll possess a striking confidence that's perpetuated over the long term. The longer you live in accordance with your values, the deeper and deeper this confidence will penetrate into your consciousness, and the more and more it will be naturally expressed through your thoughts and actions.

The flip side of this equation is, of course, what happens when you don't live in line with your values. If you're someone who values self-discipline yet eats ice cream despite trying to lose weight and masturbates to porn despite consciously deciding that's it's negatively affecting your life, then you're unlikely to possess a healthy self-image. You likely beat yourself up for repeatedly undermining your values and goals. And you likely express a far lower degree of natural confidence.

So the question is: *are you living in line with your values? For each of the values you listed, what are you doing to live up to it?*

To use a few of my values as an example, this is what I'm doing:

- Entrepreneurship – I've slowly built a side business around writing, publishing, and marketing books via Amazon.

- Physical strength – I lift weights three days a week and have pursued a side-career as a personal trainer to better understand how the body moves and works,

and to help other people do the same.

- Courage – I try hard to live by the saying, the thing that you fear doing is the thing you must do. For example, when I'm single I approach at least one cute girl a day, tell her that she's cute, and try to arrange a date.

- Self-discipline – I need to work on this. I oftentimes neglect practicing habits that I've chosen to incorporate into my life, like reading every day, and fail to cut out bad habits I've chosen to eliminate, like eating dairy (I'm lactose intolerant).

Go through your list now and write down what you're already doing to live in line with your values. More importantly, write down ideas for things you COULD be doing to better live in line with your values.

The above method is a general way to correct a lack of congruency in your character and grow your long-term confidence. Throughout the book I'll offer other universal ways to speed this process up and make it easier.

Before continuing I want to explore a psychological theory that lies directly in line with this idea of long-term confidence. This theory is called *self-actualization.* This theory has been studied by a wide range of psychologists in regard to a wide range of applications, but the one that relates most closely to long-term confidence was theorized by Abraham Maslow. He called it the *hierarchy of needs*.

The basic gist of this theory is that as humans we have certain basic needs that must be met before we can worry about a subsequent level of needs. And these, in turn, must be met before we can worry about the next level of needs, and so on. In other words, the different levels of his hierarchy represent what motivates us at any given point in time.

The first level of this hierarchy is **physiological needs**: air to breathe, water to drink, food to eat, sex for reproduction, and sleep for survival. If these needs are not met, we can't survive, and thus we can't really worry about anything else. After these base level needs are met, we will then be motivated to take care of our **safety**. This includes everything from physical to financial health. Once these needs are accounted for, we can then bring our attention to **love** and finding a sense of belonging. This can be found through a combination of friends, family, and sexual partners. And that covers the first three levels of Maslow's hierarchy.

The fourth level is **esteem** – the need to feel respected. And this is the level that relates to confidence – more specifically, long-term confidence. Maslow divides this level into two distinct versions of esteem: "higher" and "lower" esteem. The "lower" version is defined by the need for recognition, fame, and attention from other people – in other words, self-esteem derived from external sources. He notes that this is markedly less reliable and more fragile than the "higher" version, which is defined by the need to embody the things that you value, otherwise known as self-respect. This "higher" version takes precedence over the "lower" version because it relies on an inner competence that's developed over time, as opposed to superficial and temporary titles or praises from other people that will inevitably pass with time.

And this is exactly what I'm talking about when I describe long-term confidence and what it takes to build a strong self-esteem that's rooted deeply in your character, and safe from the abrasions and challenges of everyday life. By ensuring that you're acting in line with your values, you'll inevitability develop this rock hard confidence before long.

If you're curious, there is a fifth and final level to Abraham's hierarchy. It's called **self-actualization,** and it's marked by the need to realize your full potential. Maslow estimated that even less than one percent of adults ever reach this level of existence. They simply aren't able to fulfill all the needs we have just covered, from their base physiological needs all the way through their self-esteem. But those that are able to get past the level of esteem, he believes, will naturally develop a deep burning desire to become everything that they're capable of becoming.

A couple examples of people Maslow thought had reached this level include Albert Einstein and Henry David Thoreau. In my opinion, reaching the point where our main motivation is pure self-improvement for the sake of reaching our full potential is the goal. But we can't get there without truly cultivating our confidence. And this is no easy task. I sincerely hope this book can assist you in this endeavor.

How Long-Term and Short-Term Confidence Interact with One Another and What This Means for You

Short-term confidence is feeling confident in your abilities in regard to a specific activity or environment. It generally manifests as a lack of negative mental chatter in the moment.

Long-term confidence is proving to yourself that you're living the life you want to, as defined by embodying the values that are most important to you. This type of confidence stays with you regardless of the environment you happen to be in.

Short-term confidence can definitely be present without long-term confidence – you can feel confident in the moment without having developed a deeply rooted long-term confidence. This can be achieved through performing a high number of repetitions in a particular activity, spending a long period of time in a specific environment, taking certain drugs, or using some of the hacks that I'll share with you shortly.

In other words, short-term confidence doesn't

require long-term confidence – and I'm sure you can easily think of multiple personal examples of this in your life or the lives of your friends. For example, I've worked with multiple guys who are extremely confident in the workplace environment, but transform into nervous introverts in almost any other public place. Think of a bouncer who struts around the nightclub like he's the king, but can't hold his head up in public during the day.

And what about if you're able to successfully develop strong long-term confidence by acting in line with your values? What does this do for you? Does it guarantee short-term confidence? I've by no means been able to successfully embody everything I value, but with a conscious effort over the past handful of years I've certainly made large strides in this area. I'm also happy to have befriended multiple guys who've truly come into their own. They do a commendable job of practicing the values that they preach.

I've found that the main effect of developing long-term confidence is making you very comfortable in your own skin. I tend to maintain a clear conscience that's not weighed down by anxiety or guilt, because I feel like I'm doing a good job practicing the things that I value and preach. And while I most definitely cannot step into any situation and immediately assume stone-cold confidence, I'm undoubtedly not as nervous or anxious as I would've been just a few years ago when entering a similar situation. I'm also able to navigate past these initial nerves and doubts at a much quicker pace.

A recent example of this in my life relates to starting a new job. Two years ago, when I decided to begin working as a personal trainer on the side, I set my mind on working for a particular luxury gym. If I was going to start training, I wanted to do it right – in an awesome facility full of people who could afford to be my clients. After countless phone calls and resume drop-offs, I got an interview, and soon after got the job.

The first day of work was really fucking intimidating. Trainers are territorial by nature. Every new trainer represents another mouth to feed, and less potential clients for the existing crew of trainers at the gym. People weren't overly friendly or helpful. Approaching the trainers and attempting to build rapport with them was nerve-racking. Approaching the members and soliciting my services was equally challenging.

Fast forward two years and I just changed gyms. With this change came the need to re-acclimate myself to a new set of trainers and gym members. This time around, it went quite smoothly. Not altogether painless, but far easier than the first time around. While you can attribute part of this to repetition – the fact that I had to make a similar adjustment two years ago – I firmly believe the main reason it was easier this time was the amount of long-term confidence that I've developed since then.

That being said, long-term confidence is undoubtedly more valuable than its short-term counterpart. And therefore, developing this more permanent form of confidence should be our primary goal. However, it takes time. Methods to speed up this process and "hacks" to quickly assume short-term confidence are therefore invaluable to our growth and success. While the majority of hacks you'll find inside are "quick-fix" type things that focus on your short-term confidence, it's important not to lose sight of this fact.

How This Book Will Give You the Solution to Both Short-Term and Long-Term Confidence

This book is organized into a list of 23 confidence "hacks" or strategies. Each chapter represents one item on this list. For each one, I'll offer a related anecdote or study, classify it as it pertains to long-term or short-term confidence, describe how it's meant to be used, and then offer advice on when it's most effectively put to use.

The original list I brainstormed had about 40 hacks, but I wanted to stay true to the "confidence hacks" title. And so I cut out some items that didn't really deal with confidence, but just positive habits in general. I also had to cut a few that I believed to be true, yet couldn't find research to corroborate.

The idea is that several, if not most of these ideas will resonate with you, and that you'll be excited to incorporate them into your life as soon as possible. The "hacks" included range from mental thought routines that can be done in a matter of seconds when you wake up in the morning, to physical routines you can complete in mere minutes when you need to blow off some steam, to simple ways to review your path in life.

By carefully selecting the "hacks" most relevant to your personality and current life situation, and then practicing them when applicable, I firmly believe you'll notice an immediate boost in confidence.

Some will assist you in bringing your actions in line with your values and developing true long-term confidence. Others are to be used in the moment and help you turn off the negative mental chatter that prevents you from tackling a particular situation with decisiveness and self-assuredness.

Because there are so many techniques inside this book, there's a danger of information overload – that you'll be overwhelmed by the many possibilities and adopt none of them as a result. To avoid this trap, I suggest selecting no more than two or three "hacks" at a time, and then testing them in your life over the course of several days.

Once you've tried one out, determine whether or not it's something that works for you and that you can see yourself continuing to use in the future. If it is, then hold onto it. If not, ditch it and replace it with another "hack". Realistically you'll only be able to incorporate a small handful of these into your life.

At the end of the book I'll review a way to "stack" a series of habits together so that you can effectively test multiple hacks at once. Stacking them like this makes them more practical to actually use, and it also makes them far more powerful. For me this is where the real value lies, and I wish I could jump right into it, but without knowing the hacks themselves, talking about stacking them is rather inefficient.

With that being said, please use what's written on the following pages to cultivate a strong self-confidence. I truly believe there are very few things more important in this life.

1. The Secret to Transforming Limiting Beliefs into Empowering Ones

When I self-published my first book, it was done as an experiment, not with the intention of making money. But it did make money. However, at the time, I believed that my career as a software engineer was, well, my career.

I didn't believe I could turn writing and marketing books into a full time profession. Writing papers and reading books were my least favorite activities in school, after all. I wrote that first book purely for the ego-boost that came along with being able to say I was a published author (it didn't end up being much of a boost, to be honest).

But, even after seeing a substantial amount of revenue from this initial experiment, I put my head back down and continued the nine to five grind in my office cubicle. The funny thing is I always wanted to be an entrepreneur who made his own living. However, despite seeing evidence that I was on the cusp of being able to do this, I backed down.

Why did I do this? Simple: I had a major limiting belief. I believed that I wasn't "good" or "experienced" enough to be an entrepreneur yet. I thought that making the move to running my own business was something I'd do sometime "down the line," but not yet. In short, I wasn't confident in my ability to make a living on my own.

I overcame this limiting belief over time. I eventually decided to write and release another book. And then another. And another. Each time, I paid more and more attention to how Amazon markets products internally. I also improved my writing with each release. I figured out that getting a big initial wave of sales and reviews causes Amazon to place my books at the top of relevant search results, on the best seller charts, and in the "customers also bought section" of similar books. This led me to focusing on building my email list so that I have a solid initial crowd of potential buyers when I release a new book. In fact, the most recent book I released – "Write Book, Make Money" – details my findings and the method I've developed for making a living writing and selling books on Amazon.

Now, while I still work part time for a gym as a personal trainer, I make the vast majority of my money through my website **HowToBeast.com** and my book sales. I fully believe that I can survive solely on the money I make from my own business endeavors. And this belief has given me the confidence to devote more and more of my time to my business, and less and less of my time to working for other people. But I didn't have this confidence until I transformed my limiting belief into an empowering one.

Hack 1: Reframing

The stories that we tell ourselves directly impact our reality. If you tell yourself that you're a worthless pile of shit that can't get a job, this belief will manifest itself in how you carry yourself in your interviews. And then you won't get an offer, because you came across as a worthless pile of shit. And this outcome will then give you more of a reason to continue believing your limiting belief. And this limiting belief will continue to sabotage your potential.

The same goes for your ability to attract women or your ability to sell a product or service. If you see yourself as a failure or believe that you're unable to do something, then you're likely to act that way. And when you act that way, you're likely to continue feeling inadequate. You must break this cycle and replace your limiting belief with an empowering one. You must change the story you're telling yourself from one of failure to one of success.

Reframing is the most effective way to do this. Reframing is a technique where you identify a limiting belief that you have, think of a different way to interpret the experiences that led you to adopt this belief, and then consciously form a new belief that motivates rather than drains or depresses you.

Doing this effectively enhances both your short-term and long-term confidence. It enhances your short-term confidence by removing the negative thoughts and beliefs you have in regard to a particular activity, like going to a job interview. It enhances your long-term confidence by allowing you to re-structure any beliefs you may have that are undermining your ability to live in line with your values.

To effectively reframe, you must consciously scan your brain for any limiting beliefs you might have and write them down. You can also catch yourself thinking these things in the moment.

Once you've written them down, you need to explore why you feel the way you do. Maybe you think you can't get a job because none of your friends have gotten jobs. Maybe you've gotten fired from your last three jobs. Maybe your parents struggle to maintain employment. Whatever the reason, write it down. The same goes for why you can't get a girlfriend, why you can't change careers, or any other limiting belief.

Finally you need to construct your new belief. This should take into account the reason you thought of for why you have the limiting belief, and then put a positive spin on it. For example "While I've been fired from my last three jobs (*the reason*), I've actually learned from my mistakes and gotten experience working at three different places as a result. I can use this experience and knowledge to my advantage in my interviews (*the reframed positive belief*)."

For my entrepreneurial pursuits, the limiting belief was that I wasn't ready to be an entrepreneur. The reasoning behind this belief was that I was young and would likely fail at my first attempts at entrepreneurship. The empowering belief that I developed over time acknowledged that many young people start profitable businesses and that if I failed, I could always return to a traditional career. This gave – and still gives – me the confidence to try new things in my business and move forward. I only wish that I'd consciously reframed this limiting belief when it arose, instead of slowly doing so over the course of several years.

2. A Simple Method to Literally Rewire Your Brain to Be More Confident

If I told you that there's one activity you can perform in a matter of minutes that's been scientifically proven to:

- Boost your immune system

- Lower your blood pressure

- Improve your digestive tract

...would you be likely to do it?

A study performed at the Maharishi International University in 1981 even found that participating in this particular activity led to "increases in intelligence and increased social self-confidence, sociability, general psychological health, and social maturity" (7).

With all of this evidence backing up such a simple practice, why would you NOT do it?

What I'm talking about is meditation, by the way. And my personal experience definitely falls in line with the various claims of these studies. After meditating I immediately feel like any stress has been lifted off my back and I can continue the rest of the day with a focused, confident attitude. And these are just the short-term, acute effects.

A recent study determined that meditating can actually grow and shrink grey matter in different areas of your brain over time. The study was performed by researchers at Harvard and Mass General Hospital (6).

The study measured the density of gray matter in subjects' brains using MRI scans. The measurements were taken before and after an eight week period of daily meditation. Some subjects did not meditate, while others meditated for roughly a half hour per day. The MRI brain scans for those that did not didn't change over the eight week period. The scans for those that did meditate, however, did change. And they changed in a profound way.

The concentration of gray matter in several key areas had increased. Those areas included the hippocampus (a brain structure important for learning, memory, and the regulation of emotions) and other areas associated with remembering the past, imagining the future, introspection, and empathy. Furthermore, the concentration of gray matter had actually decreased in the amygdala, a region associated with anxiety, fear, and stress.

In other words, meditation can literally cause lasting

changes to the very structure of your brain. And these changes can boost your memory, learning, and emotional capabilities all while decreasing anxiety and stress. For a man who means to improve his confidence and dominate life, these changes can make the difference between success and failure. All too often our emotions and our anxieties get the best of us and cripple our ability to cut through the bullshit, perform, and move forward. Meditation can fix this - and quite literally so.

Hack 2: Breath-Based Meditation

Because of the reasoning laid out directly above, this hack improves both your short-term and long-term confidence. It removes stress and anxiety to help you eliminate negative mental chatter in the short-term and actually changes your brain to help you be more self-aware in the long-term. This will, in turn, allow you to better monitor how you're living and how closely your actions fall in line with your values.

You should ideally incorporate meditation into your life on a daily basis. It should only take you five or ten minutes to complete. And if that seems like a long time, you need to ask yourself if what you'd otherwise be doing for those few minutes could possibly offer you the potential benefits that meditation does.

I suggest that you meditate once per day at the time of day that you tend to feel the most stressed out.

For me this is about halfway through the day, in the afternoon, after working from home for hours, but before heading in to the gym to train clients.

All you need to do is find a quiet place where you can sit or lie down in a comfortable position. Then simply close your eyes and begin breathing through your nose. When you inhale, focus on breathing deep into your belly so that it rises as you breathe. When you exhale, do so fully so that all of your breath leaves your body and you can feel your belly button sink in towards your spine. Set a timer on your phone for five or ten minutes and simply focus on the sensations of inhalation and exhalation for that time period. When you get distracted and start thinking about something else, don't panic or get frustrated, just accept it and return your thoughts to your breathing.

Alternatively you can follow along with this guided meditation I put together for YouTube:
http://youtu.be/yKD-IrXhYSc

This will be difficult and probably not-so-enjoyable at first. But I promise that it will get more and more beneficial and easy to do as you continue. There's a reason that so many people, from professional and Olympic athletes to US marines, have incorporated meditation into their daily routines... You'd be silly not to.

3. A Simple Affirmation to Rapidly Develop Your Sense of Self-Worth

I've grown to love myself. As egotistical as that may sound, I genuinely admire and respect the person I've become. But it wasn't always so.

How'd I get here? All of the self-improvement, business-building, dating, weight-lifting, dieting, and traveling definitely helped. I can't deny that truly beginning to live up to some of my values assisted me in this transformation.

But the truth is that there's a book I read about three years ago that offered the closest thing to a quick-fix to self-esteem that I've ever encountered. The book's called *Love Yourself Like Your Life Depends On It* and it's written by Kamal Ravikant. It's only 68 pages long, but it has over 1,000 glowing reviews on Amazon.

If you read my previous book *The Book of Alpha*, then this hack won't be anything new to you. I raved about it then, and I'm about to do it again. It would be a sin not to include it in a book titled *Confidence Hacks*.

The essence of the book is that you ought to constantly remind yourself that you love yourself by telling yourself exactly that: "I love myself". This may seem silly, but affirmations have been studied and proven to have lasting effects on our mental programming (8, 9).

I don't believe that scientists have figured out exactly how affirmations change or re-wire our brains, but the basic idea is that by telling yourself something over and over you slowly ingrain it as a reality in your unconscious. By suggesting something over and over, eventually your brain begins to accept it as the truth. And my experience with the "I love myself" affirmation confirms this notion.

I've used it when I've been feeling down about a number of things. Whether it's a recent breakup that's left me feeling dejected or a nasty review on one of my published books that's left me questioning my ability as a writer, this affirmation has saved me over and over again.

When I repeat it to myself, I quickly experience a noticeable relief. It doesn't matter that she left me because I love myself. And that's enough. I might miss her love and her company, but I don't need it. I only need my own love.

It doesn't matter if you think this book is a pile of shit, because I love myself. And that's enough. I might be disappointed it didn't help you, but I don't need your validation. I sure do *want* it, but I only *need* my own.

Hack 3: "I Love Myself" Affirmation

This hack is unique. It boosts your long-term confidence, but does so in an extremely short timeframe. It works to make you more comfortable with your current self. When used effectively it can quickly instill a sense of self-worth in your character.

By telling yourself that you love yourself you 'trick' your mind into ceasing to look for validation from external sources like people and job titles. You replace this yearning for validation with one that comes from within. This is invaluable. And extremely powerful.

I tend to only use this hack when needed. However, in the past I've used it every morning and seen powerful results. As I write this I'm re-committing to incorporating it on a daily basis. There's no reason not to.

Depending on where you are, either say "I love myself" out loud or in your head (if you're in public). Repeat it ten or twenty times. If you're at home, I recommend doing it in front of a mirror, staring into your own eyes.

This technique is powerful, and it may be uncomfortable at first. The author of the aforementioned book even admits to crying when he first tried to do it. But I promise that it's worked for me, and I highly recommend you use it too.

4. How to Design Your Own Powerful Affirmations to Boost Situational Confidence

As we explored in the previous chapter, affirmations are proven to work. You can successfully ingrain a belief in your subconscious through conscious repetition. And while that specific affirmation is the most impactful and universal confidence-inducing one I've ever encountered, the possibilities are nearly endless.

I'll give you an example of an affirmation I used just this morning to great effect. I've been pushing my strength in the gym a lot lately, and one of the toughest exercises that I'm working on improving is the barbell back squat. This is the traditional squat where you place a barbell with weights on it onto your upper back, squat down, and then stand back up.

Over a few months I had been working on my three rep max – lifting the most weight I could handle for three full repetitions. I topped out at around 315 pounds. A few weeks ago I decided to switch and begin working on my six rep max. This is a common technique in the world of weight lifting that's used to apply a different stimulus to the body in hopes of achieving an increase in strength – whether that's through an increase in muscle mass or an improvement in your nervous system's ability to perform the movement.

This morning I was attempting 300 pounds for six repetitions. This would be a new six rep max, and nearly equal to my previous three rep max. My first thought was "I'm fucked, there's no way I'm getting this up." In fact, last week I was barely able to complete six reps with 295 pounds.

I recognized that my doubt would cripple my ability to successfully get to six repetitions, and so I applied a basic affirmation that I use in similar self-doubting situations. I took a series of deep breaths, closed my eyes, and muttered "I got this shit" under my breaths, over and over again. Within a matter of twenty seconds, I was hyped up and went for it.

Needless to say, I was able to complete all six reps – not with ease, no, I struggled a lot. But I was able to do them all. I'm positive I wouldn't have been able to without the help of the "I got this shit" affirmation. Sure, my body's physical ability is a limit in itself, but we tend to limit ourselves mentally when it comes to intense physical challenges.

The famous bodybuilder Ronnie Coleman used to use a similar affirmation before attempting personal records. He would smile and say "ain't nothing but a peanut" to trick himself into believing he was about to lift a relatively light weight.

Hack 4: Situational Affirmations

One of the most powerful ways to boost short-term confidence is through situational affirmations. They do absolutely nothing for developing long-term self-esteem but they are extremely effective at getting rid of negative self-talk in the moment.

Whenever you catch yourself doubting your ability, recognize it, and then coin an affirmation about how you can overcome whatever obstacle or test you're about to face. A few examples of situation affirmations I use are:

- "I got this shit": Used to convince myself I can, in fact, do something. It could be lifting a heavy weight, approaching a girl, or walking into my manager's office to get something off my chest.

- "It's just bitches": This is not meant to be demeaning to women. Rather, I use this to remind myself that women are just a single part of my life when I find myself stressing about a girlfriend, an ex, a prospect, or something similar.

- "No, I won't": I use this when facing a situation where it'll be difficult to tell someone no to something.

Yes, I tend to include profanity in my affirmations – it makes them more powerful for me. But pick and create some that make sense for you. Also, feel free to steal mine.

5. The Easiest Way to Convey Confidence in All of Your Social Interactions

What's the first thing people notice when they meet you? First impressions are powerful – so powerful that countless studies have proven people tend to make up their minds about someone or something within a matter of milliseconds of exposure to it.

A 2006 study at Princeton University found that people's inferences about someone's attractiveness, likeability, trustworthiness, competence, and aggressiveness are made up after a mere 100 milliseconds of viewing their face. Allowing the participants to view the faces without time constraints rarely changed their judgments (10).

So, I ask you again, what's the first thing people notice about you? You want it to be something good – something that leads them to respect and like you. Or maybe you don't. At the very least, if you're reading this book, you want it to be something that reflects the confidence you mean to embody.

I can tell you from my personal experience that one of the first things people notice about me – or at least that's what they've told me – is my eye contact. I recall one time I was meeting with an attractive female employee at a previous job. After being in her office for a couple of minutes – this being the first time that we'd met – she blushed, looked down at the floor, and said, "wow, you have extremely intense eye contact." The fact that this interrupted the purpose of our meeting and that we hardly knew each other demonstrates what strong eye contact can accomplish.

Another time this was recently mentioned to me was by my current girlfriend. One day she asked me what the first thing I noticed about her was. I answered and then asked her the same. She immediately replied that it was my powerful eye contact. She added that was one of the first things that attracted her to me.

I used to have terrible eye contact. I remember barely being able to look people in the eyes in stressful situations, whether it was a girl I was talking to or my basketball coach. And these were always times when I was far from confident.

Interestingly enough, there are plenty of studies that back up the notion that eye contact correlates highly with a person's confidence. A recent 2010 study surveyed a group of American college students. The students, both male and female, were randomly assigned to one of six groups, each of which viewed a particular minute long video. The videos each contained a model that made eye contact with the camera. They were different because half of the videos contained a male model and the other half contained a female model (were there only two models? If not change "a male model" to "male models" and "a female model" to "female models." As it is, this is unclear to me). The other difference between the videos was that the models held eye contact for varying periods of time.

After viewing the videos, subjects were tested by being asked to complete self-esteem assessments as if they were the models in the videos they had watched. The results were conclusive: self-esteem scores increased significantly with the duration of eye contact (11). People simply perceive eye contact and interpret it as a measure of self-esteem.

Hack 5: Powerful Eye Contact

Imagine a man with an intimidating build and superb posture entering the room you're currently in. He slowly walks up to you, asks a question, and engages you in conversation. But he's unable to maintain eye contact for more than two or three seconds. When he entered the room and moved to approach you, you undoubtedly felt his masculine presence and perceived a strong sense of confidence. However, as soon as you met him face to face and began speaking with him, your perception of him quickly changed. He was no longer a badass alpha male, but rather just another insecure man.

While that example was rather obvious and extreme, eye contact plays a huge role in your everyday life. It affects how you feel during any given interaction, and it affects how everyone else perceives you. Without being able to skillfully maintain – and break – eye contact, it doesn't matter how straight you stand up or how thick your back is; you'll still fail to create a powerful presence.

Good eye contact signals confidence and builds comfort. It says I'm comfortable looking into your eyes and speaking with you. Bad eye contact signals weakness and breaks rapport. It says I'm a nervous little boy.

But good eye contact is more complicated than staring at someone like you're playing that game where the first person who blinks loses. When you practice this type of eye contact, it comes off as creepy, like you're a serial killer or child molester. It makes the other person think you're trying to intimidate them – or just socially unaware.

By the same token, failing to meet the other person's gaze – or immediately looking away when eye contact is made – is also terrible. This is more common. It signals a lack of confidence and shows that you're nervous or intimidated by the person you're speaking with.

The secret to mastering eye contact is to maintain it for slightly longer than the other person can. This shows confidence, but also social intelligence. It says I'm in charge of this conversation, but I'm not trying to creep you out.

The second piece to mastering eye contact is knowing how to break it. This is pretty simple: when you break eye contact, look away to the sides of the person you're speaking with, as if you're thinking or picturing something in your head. Don't look down - this shows weakness and submission.

These rules should be applied to any situation. When you're talking to your boss, firm eye contact lets him know you're not his little puppy and should be taken seriously. When you're talking to your inferior, it acknowledges their presence, but also demands respect. When you're talking to a cute girl, it builds comfort, but also leads the interaction to increasingly seductive and intense eye contact. In short, it's an unavoidable part of any interaction, and you'd be a fool not to consciously master it and use it to your advantage.

I'll add that this hack improves short-term confidence. Even if you're not feeling confident in the moment, maintaining strong eye contact will give your confidence a boost. This is because the other person's perception of you directly affects how they treat you. And this in turn feeds into how you act. They'll recognize your strong eye contact, associate it with your being a confident man, and treat you as such. When they treat you like a respectable man, you'll be more inclined to act like one. In other words, it creates a self-fulfilling prophecy of confidence.

6. The Quickest Way to Build Rapport and Assume a Positive, Social Mindset

This chapter falls directly in line with the previous one on eye contact. While strong eye contact will instantly exude confidence, there's a flip side to the coin. And that is that you may come off as intimidating or standoffish if you don't apply the eye contact properly. As we explored in the previous chapter, first impressions usually don't change – so this particular hack is of the utmost importance.

Imagine a strong confident looking man shaking your hand firmly while maintaining eye contact. His lip is curled aggressively. What do you think about him? I'm going to go out on a limb and say that you'd probably assume he's in a bad mood or just an aggressive person.

Now imagine the same scenario except this time he's smiling. This slight change will likely implant a significantly different perception of the man in your mind. Rather than a cocky asshole, he's now confident but also friendly and approachable. Depending on what you want to project, you should present yourself accordingly.

That being said, based on my personal experience and the research I conducted while writing this book, it's probably best to smile. There's conclusive evidence that supports the notion that smiling exudes both confidence and friendliness, which will lead to people treating you more favorably. And possibly more importantly, studies have shown that smiling actually makes you feel happier and more confident. In other words, smiling kills two big birds with one little stone.

One study presented a group of 133 Chinese college students with photos of men and women. The people in some of the photos were smiling, while others were not. They were then asked to evaluate the people in the photos. The people who were smiling in the photos were evaluated more positively. Moreover the students assumed the smiling people to be more intelligent, and even professed to experience warmer feelings while viewing them (12).

This only confirms the obvious: simply adjusting your facial muscles and smiling projects a confident image to everyone you interact with that you'd be silly not to take advantage of.

The added benefit that makes smiling even more worthwhile is the internal effect it's been proven to produce. A study done by Paul Ekman in 1996 sheds light on this phenomenon. Ekman is a famous American psychologist whose career has been marked by his obsession with the study of emotions and how they relate to facial expressions. In this particular study he was trying to determine if instructing a person to smile would have a positive influence on both his interpersonal relationships as well as his actually feelings.

What he found was that it doesn't really matter whether we smile because are genuinely happy or just because we are instructed to – both result in similar brain activity, and both are accompanied by a positive, happy emotional state (13).

Other similar studies have confirmed the same thing. One measured the emotional response while subjects made the long 'e' sound (to mimic the characteristics of a smile) versus when they held the long 'u' sound (to mimic the characteristics of a pout). While they didn't know what was going on, they reported feeling good after making the 'e' sound and feeling bad after making the 'u' sound.

Another study performed a similar test except they had subjects hold pens between their teeth, either protruding outwards to mimic pouting or held lengthwise to mimic smiling. The results were the same: smiling made the subjects feel happier.

Hack 6: Conscious Smiling

This hack is meant to boost short-term confidence by making you feel happier, as well as changing how you're perceived. When you feel happier, you'll naturally experience less negative thoughts and doubts – you'll be more confident. And when you're perceived as a happier person, people will treat you more favorably. And, as we covered with eye contact, this in turn will lead to them feeding you positive energy that will build your confidence in the moment.

To implement this hack, simply start smiling more. Right now you can experiment with how different types of smiles affect how you feel. Try grinning just slightly, and then try a big cheesy photographic smile. Then try something in between. Feel how each smile changes your emotional state.

Now do this in public situations. Notice how people react to you when you smile at them as you walk by. They will tend to smile back, and probably even offer a greeting. It doesn't matter if you're passing a co-worker in the office, a stranger on the street, or just walking into Starbucks to meet someone for coffee. Smiling will always generate positive responses.

The applications are literally endless. Smiling while flirting will generate more attraction. Smiling while publicly speaking will build more rapport with the audience. Apply this hack now, and apply it often.

7. A Shocking Way to Use Your Own Death as Motivation to Live a Bolder, More Confident Life

Do you often think about death?

More specifically, do you ever contemplate your own death?

These may seem like morbid and depressing questions, and at the surface they are, but a lot can be achieved by simply thinking about your own death. And there are many studies that support this notion.

In 2011, a study was published in the journal *Self and Identity*. In this study, researchers experimented on a group of female subjects. They wanted to test the terror management model in regard to health. In other words, they wanted to answer the following question: are we more likely to engage in healthy, empowering activities after consciously thinking about death? Does death motivate us to live healthier lives?

To test this hypothesis they split these women into

groups to see if having some of them think about death could increase the likelihood that they would perform breast cancer self-exams. They discovered that they were far more likely to perform these exams after being exposed to reminders of death (2). Their conclusion: terror management is an effective tool for causing us to live healthier lives.

Another relevant article was published in 2012 in the journal *Personality and Social Psychology Review*. In this article, the researchers performed an in-depth analysis on all recent studies on the topic of how thinking about death can affect our lives (4).

One study they reviewed examined people's behaviors, and how they change when they're near cemeteries. Actors interacted with unsuspecting subjects right next to a cemetery, with the graves in plain sight. They fumbled and dropped some papers right in front of these people, and then waited to see if they offered any help picking them up. They then repeated this experiment a few blocks away, out of sight of the cemetery, with a new set of subjects. The results of this study were conclusive: the subjects at the cemetery test site were over 40% more likely to offer their help to the actors.

The conclusion offered by this 2012 article was as follows: "The awareness of mortality can motivate people to enhance their physical health and prioritize growth-oriented goals, live up to positive standards and beliefs, build supportive relationships and encourage the development of peaceful, charitable communities, and foster open-minded and growth-oriented behaviors." In other words, being reminded of death can vastly improve our lives.

Hack 7: Death-Based Meditation

This hack will primarily help you improve your long-term confidence. When you think about death, you'll be motivated to make better use of the time you have left to live. This means you'll be more likely to prioritize the things that you value. And, as we explored in the introduction, prioritizing your values is what manifests a strong sense of self-esteem and self-respect over the long term.

The question, of course, is how exactly should you go about contemplating death? The techniques used in the above studies varied a lot, and so it's evident that there's not a strict method that you must follow. But I'll offer you one that's been useful to me and that always leaves me feeling motivated to embrace the life that I do have left to live.

The technique I'm about to detail varies slightly from the studies above because it prompts you to consider your own death, as opposed to just death in general. This can be more effective. In a 2011 study published in the journal *Psychological Science*, researchers tested to see how likely people were to donate blood depending on whether or not they thought about death, and whether or not they were told that blood donations were urgently needed for patients.

They found that subjects who contemplated their own deaths, as opposed to just death in general, were more willing to take action and donate blood, regardless of whether they were told that blood donations were in demand or not (5). They concluded that thinking about their own deaths specifically "enables people to integrate the idea of death into their lives more fully."

With that said, the technique that I'll offer you comes from a type of traditional meditation practiced by Tibetan Buddhist monks. It's called the *Nine Point Death Meditation*. In Buddhism, there exists a firm belief that everything is impermanent – everything is temporary from your possessions and relationships all the way to your life. And they've found that reminding yourself of your own death is an extremely effective way of integrating this belief into your everyday actions.

To use this meditation, begin by assuming a comfortable posture. Sitting with your legs crossed or lying on your back are two good options. Now begin to breathe deeply – full breaths all the way down into your belly. Count ten breaths to calm your nerves and prepare yourself for the meditation.

Finally, read the following truths one-by-one, closing your eyes in between each to let them sink in and think of any relatable experiences or memories that you have (e.g. near death experiences, deaths of friends or family members, news stories, etc.):

Truth 1: Death is certain

1. We cannot escape death

2. Each moment we're alive brings us one step closer to death

3. Death comes in a single instant and is unexpected

Conclusion: You must live a good life that's in line with your values

Truth 2: The time of death is uncertain

4. The duration of our lives is unpredictable

5. There are more causes for death than causes for life

6. The human body is extremely fragile

Conclusion: You must begin living in line with your values immediately

Truth 3: The only thing that can help you at the time of death is your mental and spiritual development

7. Wealth we've accumulated can't help

8. Friends and family can't help

9. Our bodies can't help

Conclusion: Don't get distracted or obsessed with material things or other people – you alone are responsible for your confidence, growth, and development

After practicing this meditation you shouldn't feel gloomy and depressed by the prospect of dying. Rather, you should feel confident and motivated to stop making excuses and start living the good life right now.

8. How to Release Pent Up Anger and Instantly Eliminate Negative Mental Chatter

One day not so long ago I found myself in a very angry place. I'd made plans with a girl I'd been dating and when I called to confirm them, she didn't answer. I never received a text or call back.

Normally, this wouldn't bother me. But I'd been dating her for a couple months at that point – she wasn't just some random girl. And I also had nothing else to do that day. And so I sat there idly and let my thoughts and emotions spiral out of control inside of me.

I felt something I rarely do – anger. It still doesn't logically make sense to me why this combination of circumstances made me angry, but it definitely did. I tend not to invest too much in women psychologically. It's too easy to make women the biggest source of stress in your life. And if things don't work out, I've proven to myself that finding and dating new girls is something I'm more than capable of doing. I don't say this to brag, because I know guys far more skilled with women than myself.

I say this because it still perplexes me why I felt this way about this particular girl on that particular day. I suppose I really liked her.

Anyway, in the past when I found myself angry or frustrated, I tended to yell or scream to release the tension. Maybe I'd stomp my feet, too. Yes, this may seem childish to you, but there's something to be said about how efficiently kids can deal with their emotions by practicing this type of behavior.

On this particular day, I did something slightly different, and the result was so powerful that I continue to use it to this day. It's like a potent drug made to cure anger and frustration.

Hack 8: Angry Shadow Boxing

This hack is meant to boost your short-term confidence by eliminating angry thoughts. When left unchecked, angry thoughts can drown out all other mental chatter and 'take over' your brain.

By releasing your anger externally, you allow these thoughts to exit your head. Once they've gone, you can proceed with the tranquility necessary to keep your mind quiet and be confident in the moment.

Angry shadow boxing combines the effective childish behavior of screaming with the art of shadow boxing. Don't worry: you don't need to know how to box to use this hack.

The basic idea of shadow boxing is to find some open space where you can move around a little and then pretend you're in a fight. You want to visualize an opponent and then proceed to throw punches, kicks, elbows, and knees at him while you move around. This is a technique used by nearly all professional and amateur fighters as a warm-up or to prepare for a fight.

If you've never learned how to properly stand, punch, or kick, here are a few basic tips. I've also referenced a YouTube video that does a good job of demonstrating proper technique.

Stance: Stand with your feet shoulder width apart and your dominant leg moved slightly back. Your front foot should be flat and your back foot should be raised so that you're on the ball of your foot. Your weight should be evenly distributed between your feet. Your hands should be held up in fists, at approximately jaw level, to protect your face. Finally, your chin should be tucked to protect your head – it's easiest to get knocked out when you're hit on the chin, especially with an upper cut from below.

Punch: Begin with your hands in fists in the above position. Make sure your thumbs are wrapped around your other fingers just below the knuckles, as opposed to inside of your other fingers. To punch, step through your feet, twisting through your hips to generate momentum, and then extend your arm quickly, twisting your fist from vertical to horizontal.

Finish by quickly retracting it back to your jaw, right where it came from.

This video does a phenomenal job of demonstrating how to stand and how to punch. Combining these two things is enough to begin shadow boxing: **https://www.youtube.com/watch?v=MY9po0amDtg**

You're going to do this with the caveat that you're going to yell whatever's on your mind as you punch and kick the air in front of you. Typical things I yell include "fuck you" and "motherfucker." I know that's kind of humorous to read silently in a book, but the truth is that if you're embracing your angry emotions as you go, this is going to feel extremely therapeutic.

I realize that this hack is going to sound childish or silly to some readers. I accept that fact, and the judgment that comes along with it. However, most people allow societal norms to pressure them into barricading themselves behind layers and layers of emotional and mental baggage as they grow older. Throwing fits and screaming has been deemed childish and inappropriate. I believe this is unfortunate. Quite often, internal tension is best released through our natural tendencies, often best expressed by the temper tantrums of young children.

Use angry shadow boxing whenever you find yourself drowning in anger or frustration and I promise it will allow you to move past at least the blunt end of these negative emotions and focus on the task at hand.

9. The Only Way to Forget Something That's Eating Up Your Confidence from the Inside

I can be pretty awful when it comes to having compulsive thoughts that I can't get off my mind. Whether it's about a girl, a friend, a work project, or anything else, it's not rare for me to lie on the floor for an hour or two running through the same shitty mental loop in my head. Not only do I not make any progress in sorting out whatever's on my mind, but it also makes me feel extremely anxious. It kills my confidence for the rest of the day – or for however long it takes to clear my mind.

A few months ago, the gym I was working at was acquired by another gym. It was set to shut down. I was faced with a decision: quit working as personal trainer and focus more time on my business and my writing, get a job at another gym, or begin training on my own at a private facility.

For days, even weeks, I found myself consumed with thinking about these three options. I've always wanted to focus on my business and writing on a full time basis, but I know that not having a reason to leave my desk is dangerous. Without training, I'm afraid I would drive myself crazy working on my laptop all day, every day.

And so, if I'm going to train, should I do it on my own, or work for another gym? I'd make more per session on my own, but finding clients is easier at a gym. Also, working at a gym provides health insurance and a gym membership.

And so I straddled the fence, unable to commit to either option, and unsure which was best. Not only did this put the decision off, but it clearly affected my confidence during that time period. The fact that I couldn't make a decision left me with a constant feeling of unease in regard to the rest of my life – my diet sucked, I acted coldly towards my girlfriend, and I blew off my friends.

Hack 9: Concrete Decision Making

Finally, one day I took out a notepad and physically wrote down my decision, and the underlying reasoning: *to work part time at a new gym. This will help me maintain my mental sanity by giving me an excuse to get out of my house and off my laptop every day, and will provide me with health insurance and a gym membership at the nicest club in my area. Sure, I won't be making the most money possible with this decision, but the other value it will offer makes it worth it.*

And then I immediately stopped torturing myself and thinking through endless, hopeless loops about this particular decision. This is a technique I'd used before, but not in a while.

Since that day I've used it liberally, to great effect. Whenever I catch myself unable to get past a certain dilemma in my head, whether it's about a girl, a book I'm writing, a client at the gym, or otherwise, I take out my notebook, where I have a page with the word "Decisions" written across the top, and then write down a decision that puts the matter to rest, and my reasoning behind why this is best for me.

This is extremely effective in keeping my mind clear and free from compulsive thoughts that would otherwise eat away at my tranquility and confidence. Do the same, and make yourself a notepad or document on your laptop, where you write down a decision whenever you catch yourself obsessing over something stupid. If it pops back into your head, just remind yourself that you've already made a decision and move on.

This hack actually improves both your short-term and long-term confidence. It obviously improves your confidence in the moment by removing compulsive thoughts that will prevent you from entering a positive, self-assured mindset. After all, how can you be confident in your abilities if you can't confidently make an important decision?

It improves your long-term confidence because if you constantly employ this technique, you're sure to act more in line with your values. This is because when you write down the reasoning for a particular decision, you bring your underlying motivations and values to a conscious level.

10. An Instant Cure for Two Big Confidence Killers (Self-Loathing and Anxiety)

Depression can strike at any time. There's always something that seems shitty in our lives. There's always something we can improve upon. And unfortunately we tend to focus on and obsess over these types of things.

Anxiety is something that I constantly struggle with. Because, for the same reasons I mentioned above, there's always something to worry about. There's always something that could turn out poorly.

Both of these common negative conditions usually stem from a feeling of lack. We convince ourselves that we lack something – whether it's female affection, money, self-confidence, a good job, cool clothes, an attractive body, or otherwise – and then we feel shitty about ourselves as a result.

I could recount endless examples of this from my life. Currently my main source of anxiety is my income situation. I'm not working the "perfect" job. I like personal training, but the inconsistent hours and scheduling nightmares that come with it both suck. I don't really like the software work I'm doing, but it pays well. And I love my website, courses, and books, but there's no clear path to where I should go next.

What I do know is that I need to drop one of these three commitments. All three of them require a lot of organization, planning, and work. They're all potential full time jobs. By holding onto all three, I'm doing all of them a disservice by not truly being able to fully focus on any of them. And this has made me feel paralyzed and shitty lately – like I can't enjoy life until the situation is resolved.

Yesterday I made a decision to quit one of them (per hack #9). And I feel better about it all now. But that's not the point. The point is that I let the problem control my feelings. I let the negativity and uncertainty drown out all of my other emotions.

If it weren't for the following confidence hack, it would've been much worse. The following activity allowed me to escape the mental trap that I found myself in quite often as a result of that predicament. It allowed me to shift from a mindset of lack and depression to a mindset of abundance and happiness.

Hack 10: Count Your Blessings

Every time I realize that I'm beating myself up about how "bad" things are, I stop myself and instead list all of the things I have that I'm grateful for. My list usually consists of things like my new apartment where I'm living alone, my new girlfriend whom I'm always looking forward to seeing, my friends who are always down to hang out, the fact that I have three jobs, the awesome gym where I work, the flexibility of the software company that allows me to work whenever I want to from home, Amazon and the opportunity it's given me to monetize my knowledge and ideas by publishing books, my health, the physical progress I've made in regard to bodybuilding over the past few years, and the mystery of life itself – to name a few.

We all have things to be thankful for. We all have assets that allow us to live the lives that we do. But it's easy to forget these things. It's easy to focus instead on what we don't have or what's not right. Practicing deliberate gratitude is the solution to this problem. We must remind ourselves of all the amazing things that we do have.

This hack improves our short-term confidence by alleviating the negative mindset that comes along with wishing that things were different, or wishing things were better. When we're feeling a sense of lack or self-pity, we tend to act accordingly. Feelings of weakness and insecurity drown out our positive emotions and make us miserable and introverted. We get in our heads. We feel badly about ourselves, and that, by definition, subverts our confidence.

By reminding ourselves of all of the things, people, and experiences that we're lucky to have, we short-circuit these emotions and instead focus on the good. We fill ourselves with a sense of abundance. We remove the doubts. We replace them with a confidence that stems from everything that we do have.

Whenever you catch yourself thinking negatively, stop and remember everything that you do have. Be grateful for it. You'll immediately feel and act more confidently.

11. A Simple Way to Stop Taking Yourself so Seriously and Stop Playing the Victim

How do you react when things don't go as you'd like? You get fired. You say something that makes the girl you're flirting with run away. Your friend cancels on you at the last minute. Your girl breaks up with you.

Most guys would act as though the weight of the world were placed on their shoulders – as though life as they'd known it had ended. As though their job, girlfriend, plan, or friend were the only thing they'd had to live for. They'd cry themselves to sleep and then bitch and moan to everyone they'd talk to for the next week or month or so. Instead of shrugging it off, learning from it, and continuing to live, they'd complain and get depressed.

This is known as playing the victim. It's when you view your existence as a burden rather than an incredible opportunity to enjoy life and accumulate new experiences. You think that everyone is out to get you and that you have little control over your own life. You're just waiting for the next bad thing to happen. One way people get trapped in this mindset is by taking themselves too fucking seriously.

When your friend fucks up it's no big deal, right? He just got rejected by three girls in a row and you're laughing your ass off and telling him to go for four. But when it happens to you, you start telling yourself that you're ugly and that girls think you're a creep. What's the difference?

The difference is that you're taking yourself way too seriously. Shit happens. Some things don't go your way. Our reactions to unwelcoming circumstances define us. When the shit hits the fan, will you curl your lip, grit your teeth, and curse the world for damning you once again? Or will you take a step back and realize that such is life, before smiling and proceeding accordingly?

In life, the people who take themselves and their circumstances way too seriously, even the wealthy and successful ones, ultimately lose. Rather than enjoying the things that they do experience, they focus on the negative and always find a way to spoil their own fun. This is not an invitation to be a lazy hippie, but rather a reminder to have fun and keep a lighthearted approach to life as you progress as a man and follow your goals.

Hack 11: Appreciate the Mystery of Life

There are surely a number of ways to remind yourself that life is great and avoid focusing on the negative. In fact, a number of the other hacks I've included in this very book will accomplish this (hack

#10 – counting your blessings, for example). But this particular hack addresses the root of this problem more effectively than any other.

The hack in question is appreciating the mystery of life and the little things about this planet that we live on. It's done by simply stopping what you're doing for a moment and looking around you.

- What do you see?

- How do these things work, live, operate, etc.?

- How did they come to be?

- How awesome is that?

Now, before you dismiss this as some hippie bullshit, let me continue.

Right now, for example, I'm looking out my window. There's a teacher leading a group of high school students down the street. At least, that's what I'm assuming because there's a high school right down the street. He's white, about 50 years old, and walking with a slight hunch in his back. His face resembles Kevin Spacey's. The students are all black. Some of them are lagging behind and joking around with each other. Others are right behind the teacher, listening attentively. I wonder where they all grew up… Probably here in Boston. I wonder what class they're in and why they're walking down the street right now.

There's a group of huge pine trees next to the sidewalk they're walking by. I wonder how old they are. Wikipedia tells me pine trees usually live anywhere from one hundred to one thousand years. That's amazing. These trees were probably there when I was born and they'll probably be there when I'm dead.

I turn to the inside of my apartment... to this very screen that I'm typing on. I consider myself technologically savvy – I work for a software company and write code after all – but I still have absolutely zero idea how humans were ever able to create high definition displays. Or even old school televisions with the wood grain finish. It's amazing, really.

...And that's a typical example of appreciating the mystery of life. What this does is get you out of your head and out of the petty problems of your life. It opens your mind to the world around you, and makes you realize how insignificant you are. And this shouldn't depress you; rather, it should take the weight of your personal issues off your shoulders, because at the end of the day it doesn't matter how many dollars you've made or if you're dating the hottest girl, life goes on anyway.

12. A Quick at-Home Full-Body Workout to Improve Posture, Strength, and Muscle Mass

One of the easiest ways to boost your confidence is through exercise. Numerous studies have measured increases in self-esteem as a result of physical exercise (14, 15). And it makes sense: exercising improves your body, and we humans are a vain race. When we look better, we're inherently going to feel better, because we really do care about how we look.

When it comes to exercise, there are two main types: aerobic and anaerobic, a.k.a. cardio and strength training. In a nutshell, cardio serves to improve the functioning of your heart and lungs, and strength training serves to improve your muscular and skeletal systems.

When it comes to confidence, the results achieved through strength training are more relevant simply because they're directly tied to how we look. Bigger arms, broader shoulders, a thicker chest, and the ability to stand up straight are all related to the ideals of strength and confidence in modern society. And I'm not talking about becoming a giant, steroid-injecting bodybuilder – just a solid, strong, self-assured man.

From my personal experience I can tell you that the effects strength training has on building confidence are profound and often understated. I could go on for hours talking about how strength training was the catalyst for my own personal transformation, but I'd rather focus on my training clients. It's quite common to see their confidence skyrocket after only a few weeks of training.

A recent example is a girl I train who's currently in high school. She's tall but tends to slouch forward terribly. This poor posture is reflected in her personality and self-esteem. When I first met her, we chatted for a bit. She could barely hold eye contact, speaking very little while slouching down into her chair. She wasn't confident, to say the least.

It's only been three weeks, but things have changed and drastically so. Her parents recently came to me and told me how much happier and confident she's become already. They asked me how this is possible.

Hack 12: Simple Strength Training

I told the parents the truth. There are two main things that have changed. Number one is her posture. It's only been a few weeks, so little muscle has been built, and little fat has been lost. Also, deeper psychological changes haven't had time to occur. She's just standing up straighter. Number two is a sense of progress. Every time we work out, she's able to do one more repetition or a little bit more weight. Progress begins a feeling of personal growth and this will make anyone feel good about themselves.

They seemed surprised that the subtle changes in her posture could have caused the large improvements they'd noticed. So I explained. First of all, when someone stands up straight they're perceived as more confident, even if they still feel shitty about themselves. Secondly, our bodies are inherently tied to our minds. When we stand up straight, hold our heads high, and expand our chests, we tend to feel confident and powerful as a result. When we roll our shoulders forward and look down to the ground, on the other hand, we tend to assume the same weak, cowering mindset that our bodies are projecting (more on this in the next chapter).

So it's a double whammy. You stand up straight, people think you're more confident, and you actually are a bit more confident. And this combined effect is powerful. The increased muscle mass, decreased body fat, and six packs abs that come with time are awesome too – don't get me wrong – but they only build on these initial benefits.

This hack is a super simple, easy, and quick training

routine that you can do at home or at the gym. It combines strength training and cardio, and focuses on building strength in functional movement patterns that will build a strong, balanced physique and improve posture.

Perform the following 4 exercises roughly every other day. Perform them as a circuit (do each exercise once and then repeat) three times through, resting only for 30 seconds in between movements. In the parentheses, I've included different variations of the exercises (listed left to right from easy to hard). Once you're able to complete 15 repetitions (without resting) of a particular variation, then move on to the next hardest one. If you're unsure of how to perform a particular exercise, Google it; these are all quite common.

1. Squats (bodyweight squat > jump squat > single leg box squat > pistol squat)

2. Push-Ups (knee push-ups > incline push-ups > push-ups > decline push-ups > clap push-ups)

3. Pull-Ups (assisted pull-ups > table pull-ups > pull-ups)

4. Sit-Ups (crunches > sit-ups with feet under weighted object > sit-ups)

13. One Weird Way to Trick Your Mind into Being More Confident

One of the keys pieces to the weight lifting routine laid out in the previous chapter is its favorable effect on posture. But what if I told you there's an even quicker way to take advantage of this aspect of weight lifting.

A recent study conducted at Columbia University investigated how powerful individuals tend to hold themselves. For example, alpha male gorillas tend to stand up tall and beat their chests. Alpha male business men tend to put their leg up on a chair or spread their hands out on a table during business meetings and take up more space. The study aimed to explain these "power poses" and their causes and effects.

The result is extremely interesting. They confirmed that holding tall, expansive poses actually changes the levels of various hormones inside our bodies when compared to cowering, closed postures. Here's what they found:

"Humans and other animals express power through open, expansive postures, and they express powerlessness through closed, contractive postures. But can these postures actually cause power? The results of this study confirmed our prediction that posing in high-power nonverbal displays (as opposed to low-power nonverbal displays) would cause neuroendocrine and behavioral changes for both male and female participants: High-power posers experienced elevations in testosterone, decreases in cortisol, and increased feelings of power and tolerance for risk; low-power posers exhibited the opposite pattern. In short, posing in displays of power caused advantaged and adaptive psychological, physiological, and behavioral changes, and these findings suggest that embodiment extends beyond mere thinking and feeling, to physiology and subsequent behavioral choices. That a person can, by assuming two simple 1-min poses, embody power and instantly become more powerful has real-world, actionable implications." (16)

In short, assuming "power poses" or expansive body language marked by expanding your chest and taking up space actually increases your testosterone levels and decreases your cortisol levels. Testosterone is a hormone responsible for things like building muscle, growing hair, and aggression. Cortisol is a hormone that's released in response to stress. In other words assuming these "power positions" will actually make you feel more powerful and less stressed.

Hack 13: Power Posing

This research discovered an amazing short-term confidence hack. Power posing will change your hormone levels and transform your mental state into one of power and leadership.

To apply this hack, simply assume a power pose and hold it for about a minute before entering a situation that requires confidence – for example, before entering a job interview or a bar for a date.

A few common power poses include:

- Standing with your legs in a wide stance and your arms spread out wide overhead (you should feel a stretch across your chest) as if you just won a race or some other competition (*this one is my favorite and really the only one that I use)

- Standing with your legs in a wide stance and your hands on your hips

- Sitting back in chair with one leg crossed over on

your opposite knee and your hands behind your neck with your elbows spread wide

These are just a few. In the end, anything that takes up space and conveys power or confidence will yield that same feeling.

14. Stand Proudly: A Quick Fix for Poor Posture

The Columbia University study on power posing offers us an extremely useful tool. By assuming powerful, expansive postures for brief periods of time, we can achieve measurable boosts in short-term confidence.

But what if I told you there's a way to maintain these benefits on a permanent basis?

There is. And it's somewhat obvious. If you can alter your body so that you assume powerful, expansive postures by default, you'll consequently adopt the same mindset by default. Integrating strength training into your life, as recommend a couple chapters ago, solves part of this equation. It strengthens your back to help you stand up straight and builds muscles like your chest and shoulders that contribute to a powerful appearance.

But there's a second part to this equation. And it works far more quickly than the strength training advice, which operates over the long-term (as it takes time for our bodies to synthesize new muscular tissue).

It won't increase your muscle mass or grant you the

numerous other benefits of exercise, but it will transform how you hold your body throughout the day. And this is important not only because people will perceive you as a more confident person when you stand up straight and hold yourself upright, which they will, but also because it will actually change how you feel inside, as seen with power posing.

Hack 14: Focused Stretching

While this hack should be practiced over the long term, it actually works to improve short-term confidence.

When it comes to stretching, we all have particular muscles that have become tight as a result of how we carry ourselves throughout the day. And stretching these muscles will improve how we move and feel.

But we're going to focus on the two areas that are responsible for weak posture in the vast majority of people today: the chest and the neck. These muscles can shorten and grow tight as a result of any activity where you lean forward, use your arms in front of you, or strain your neck forward. Common examples of such activities include typing on a computer, driving a car, or playing video games.

Because you hold yourself in a position where your shoulders roll forward, you hunch your upper back, and you strain your neck for extended periods of time, your body adapts to these circumstances. Your back muscles lengthen and weaken while your chest muscles tighten. And the result of this is the standard poor posture marked by hunching over forward.

The impact on confidence is the same as the weak poses studied by Columbia University. You close your chest and take up less space. And you adopt a similarly weak, anxious mindset as a result.

You must combat this with proper stretching of the chest and neck. Doing so effectively will counter the many modern day activities that serve to cripple your posture. It will allow you stand tall and proud. This will leak into your mentality and transform your confidence.

Perform the following the following two stretches every day to achieve better, more confident posture:

1. Standing inside of a doorframe, place your palms out to the sides and onto either side of the doorframe. Now slowly walk forward so that your arms extend behind you and you stretch your chest. Once your arms are fully straight and behind you, lean forward and experience a strong stretch in your chest. Hold this for at least 30 seconds. It should feel quite good.

2. Standing straight up, tuck your chin down to your chest and then roll your head to the left. Relaxing your neck and allowing the weight of your head to weigh it down, you should feel a slight stretch on the back right side of your neck. Let your right hand hang by your side and place your left hand on the back right side of your head. Lightly pull your head forward and to the left to deepen the stretch. Hold this for 30 seconds and then repeat it on the other side.

15. How to Turn Both Your Failures and Successes into Increased Confidence

I want to tell you a story. This story takes place last Friday in Boston.

Something I alluded to earlier is that I'm struggling to balance my time between personal training, software consulting, and growing my books and blog business.

The first two hours of my Friday were spent writing this very book. But around 11AM I had to head into the gym and work straight through to 6PM.

I'd had enough of having to commit my entire days to the gym. And so when I had a brief 30 minute break, I stopped by my manager's office. I explained to him that the variety of times I had to be at the gym simply wouldn't work for me going forward. I reminded him of my other commitments and put down a firm foot in regard to the fact that I'd only be training clients on weekday afternoons and evenings going forward. And we agreed on a solution in order to make this adjustment.

I felt great. Despite having to go back on the initial

times I'd told him I'd be available, which made for a slightly uncomfortable encounter, I would now be able to commit my mornings to my software job and my weekends to my books and blogs. A weight had been lifted from my shoulders.

That day also happened to be Halloween. I got home from the gym. My girlfriend met me there. We were to go to a Halloween party. But before we left the house, I inadvertently picked a fight. I won't go into details but I let a minor inconvenience get the best of me. This led to us leaving an hour later than planned. No big deal. Things seemed okay.

However, a few hours and a number of drinks later, the tension resurfaced. And it turned into an ugly drunk fight that ended with her sleeping on my couch. These things happen.

Hack 15: The Daily Review

The next morning, as I lay in bed, it was tough to think about anything besides the fight from last night. And thinking about it simply brought the tension and anger back into me. I was simply looping through the negative parts of the night on repeat, as we tend to do.

It wasn't until I caught myself and used this hack that I was able to move forward with a clear conscience and positive emotions.

The hack is simple. At the end of every day, before going to sleep, or at the beginning of every day, upon waking up, perform a review of the day that's just passed. Ask yourself: what did I do well that I should strive to do again? And then ask yourself: what will I do differently the next time a similar situation arises?

This allows you to pat yourself on the back for behaviors that are in line with your values. And it also allows you to acknowledge behaviors that aren't in line with your values, and analyze how you should change them the next time you're put into a similar situation. I try to think of two to three examples of each from my day.

In the case of my Friday I mentioned above, I'd say that I did well in confronting my boss about my time commitment to the gym. Rather than try to fix it on my own or create a precedent that I could work whenever they so wished, I made it a point to state my stance early on. This embodies a combination of honesty and courage that's in line with my stated values. No, it's not a super courageous move that I mean to brag about, but you should monitor all of your actions and experiences. Even the seemingly insignificant ones can have a lasting effect when repeated countless times.

When I thought about the things that I'd do differently, the obvious one that came to mind was how I handled myself with my girlfriend. When something bothered me at the beginning of the night, I let it consume me. I acted from a place of neediness and insecurity, and, rather than approaching the situation with a level head, I acted like a child whose dad had told him he couldn't have a dirt bike for Christmas (yes, that did happen to me). Next time a similar situation arises, I need to take a step back, take a few deep breaths, and realize that I do not control my girlfriend and that she's in my life for pleasure and enjoyment, so I should not turn her into a source of tension and anxiety. If things don't go as I'd like, I'll let it be known but do my best to leave it at that and move on with life.

This hack improves both short-term and long-term confidence. It improves short-term confidence by bringing a sense of tranquility to your mind. After you've reviewed your day, you can let everything go, taking only the knowledge and lessons that you extracted from the review, and leaving the bad emotions and other baggage behind. This also improves long-term confidence by giving you the opportunity to ensure that you're living in line with your values on a daily basis, and allowing you to course-correct yourself if that's not the case.

16. How to Turn off Your Mind and Sleep Soundly Every Single Night

What's the main thing that keeps you from falling asleep at night?

I honestly don't have trouble falling asleep. In fact, many of my friends joke that I'm a narcoleptic because I can literally fall asleep at a moment's notice, pretty much regardless of what time of day it is. I've lately even picked up the habit of a late morning nap. I'll wake up at about 7 or 8AM and then take a 30 minute nap around 10:30AM after a couple hours of work.

But most people I know struggle with sleep because they can't stop thinking about things. They get caught in mental loops that drive them crazy, make them anxious, and make the act of falling asleep seem more like a fantasy than a reality.

And while I don't experience this now, I definitely have in the past. One thing I've done to overcome this challenge is the following hack. It's meant to get everything on off your mind so that you can fall asleep more quickly and sleep more soundly.

If you struggle to sleep for other reasons – like consuming a lot of caffeine to late in the day or because your neighbors are throwing a party – then, well, this won't help.

Hack 16: Pre-Bed Mental Exhaustion

This hack improves short-term confidence and your health in general. When you sleep better, you feel more alert and energetic – two conditions that are almost requirements for projecting a strong, confident image.

What you are going to do is mentally exhaust yourself by getting everything that's on your mind off of it. You're going to do this by writing everything down on a sheet of paper or in a notebook that you keep by your bed.

Don't use your phone or laptop – studies have shown that viewing luminous screens before sleeping suppresses melatonin levels and can cripple your ability to sleep and even cause sleep disorders (17).

Now you can sleep soundly, knowing that you can pick up where you left off in the morning and that you aren't going to forget whatever it is you were thinking about.

17. One Thing Every Man Must Have in Order to Project Confidence and Strength

There's one thing in life that makes all the difference. If you have it, you'll be driven to succeed and this will manifest itself in all of your actions. People will recognize this drive and respect you for it.

If you don't have it, you'll feel depressed and impotent. And this will also come through in how you carry yourself. People will see a weak man who doesn't know where he's headed. They will see a man without a mission.

And that's just the thing: having a mission. Without one, your life begins to revolve around routine tasks and relationships. Rather than thinking about the next step to building your business or improving a particular skill, you'll be worrying about your girlfriend or day dreaming about playing your favorite video game when you get home.

Without a primary goal that you're working towards, the little things that are in your life for enjoyment and pleasure will turn into sources of anxiety and obsession. You need to know where you're going. It's that simple.

Recently I got all too caught up in the day to day grind. I know my mission: building and growing How To Beast (my company). I want to write articles, film videos, publish books, and create courses to reach as many men as possible. I want to research what makes us happy and confident. I want to discover hacks for getting better at skills that I'm interested in (e.g. monetizing a blog, dating, bodybuilding, etc.). I want to share my experiences and my research with as many people as possible. I want to add value to my life and to those of other people. And, honestly, I want to make money doing it.

But recently between building my personal training business at a new gym, getting in a new long-term relationship, and dealing with my family moving across the globe, I lost sight of this. Instead of having my mind focused on solving the issues and challenges that How To Beast is facing, I was drowning in doubt and anxiety. When will I see my father again? How will I build my training clientele quickly while maintaining a robust schedule that allows me time to work on How To Beast? When will I see my girl next? Have I forgotten many of my man friends in the process?

And the thing is, not only has my progress stalled, but I'm less confident and in-the-moment because of it. Not only has my revenue declined, but I'm worrying about useless shit instead of focusing on how to resurrect it.

These are the dangers of not having a primary mission.

Hack 17: The Primary Mission

This hack is not really a hack. Working towards a goal is not a hack. But it is in the sense that it boosts your short-term confidence by alleviating the stress and anxiety that come along with not having a mission. And so I must include it in this book.

It also improves your long-term confidence. If you're working towards an important goal, it's sure to be in line with your stated values. And this, by definition, will allow you to lead a more purposeful, dedicated life that naturally manifests confidence in your character.

To implement this hack into your life, simply create a mission for yourself if you don't already have one. Start by brainstorming a list of outcomes you'd like to achieve. If you're struggling, try to create a potential goal for each of the following categories:

1. Professional (getting a job, getting a promotion, changing careers, starting a business)

2. Physical (losing weight, building muscle, solving a health problem, learning a martial art, participating in a sports league, completing a *Tough Mudder* type race)

3. Adventure (hiking a mountain, visiting an exotic destination, taking a vacation)

4. Personal (meeting new women, going on a date with a cute girl, finding a girlfriend, writing a book, starting a blog, taking a programming course on CodeAcademy.com, learning a foreign language)

Don't get caught up trying to create the *perfect* goal. It doesn't exist. Just choose one thing to get started with. If you have trouble, then start with something small that you can accomplish within a matter of weeks (e.g. going on a date with a cute girl, taking one martial arts class, going to the gym three times a week for a month). Realize that it's not the specific goal that matters – it's simply the fact that you have one.

18. How to Incorporate Focus and Purpose into Your Daily Life

Last night, before I went to sleep, I couldn't get one thing off my mind. I kept thinking, "I need to film a couple of YouTube videos tomorrow."

YouTube provides one of the largest audiences for companies, bloggers, and people in general to spread their messages. The way in which we consume information is changing. Right now people are getting their news, entertainment, and education in video form more than ever before.

As of May 2014, YouTube accounted for 13.2 percent of total internet bandwidth during peak usage times (18). This number is enormous.

What this means for me is that YouTube is a must in terms of uploading videos and using it as a medium to spread my message and attract followers. Any company would be silly to NOT use YouTube right now.

Anyway, fast-forward to today. After waking up, I promptly began to generate a list of my top viewed blog posts. These are my top prospects for YouTube as they're likely to capture the largest possible number of views. This is in contrast to a normal day where I might browse the internet for an hour or so before starting to get to work.

After this, I reviewed the content of two of the posts, got dressed, grabbed my camera and mic, and headed to my rooftop to film a video on a beautiful New England fall day. After filming, I went straight to the gym and got a workout in. Afterwards I hit up the coffee shop in order to edit the videos and type another chapter of this book.

Hack 18: The Daily Goal

The purpose of this narrative is to illustrate the power of having a daily goal. When you set a goal that you mean to accomplish on a particular day, not only are you less likely to procrastinate and more likely to be productive and achieve the goal, but you're also sure to bring a strong sense of determination with you throughout the day.

This is because you're acting in line with your values on a short-term basis. Rather than drifting through the day, something that's likely to fill you with a sense of lethargy and depression, you storm forward.

People recognize this potency as well. You can easily tell the man with a mission apart from the man without one. The man with a mission is pursuing his purpose. He's happy and confident as a result. The man without a purpose, on the other hand, will often come off as weak or lost.

This hack improves your short-term confidence by instilling this potency into your character. To implement it into your life, simply identify one task that you will accomplish on each and every day.

19. The Secret to Finding Your Perfect Hair Style

Your hair has grown too long. After a month of putting it off, you finally find an hour to head to the local barbershop. You sit in line for a half hour and then the barber motions for you to take a seat in that good old comfy leather chair.

The barber asks you, "What can I do for you today?"

"Fuck!" you think. "I'll just take a regular cut, short on the sides and clippers on top."

Thirty minutes later, you walk out, hop in your car, and flip down the sun shield to check out your new cut in the mirror. "Meh," you think, "this will do".

Sound familiar? As guys, we tend not to care too much about how good our hair looks. But, once in a while, when you get a great cut, you feel pretty damn good.

We ARE vain. And our looks DO influence how we feel – more for some of us than for others. But it's worth it to get down a system to make sure that you always get a haircut that makes you feel like a boss.

Hack 19: The Perfect Haircut

This hack will improve your short-term confidence by ensuring that your hair is always on point. You'll experience that confidence boost that you get when you know you're looking good.

The idea is to get one really good haircut and then take a set of photos that you can present to barbers you visit in the future. The thing is that barbers are actually pretty good at giving you the cut you want if you give them a visual to aim for. But when you go in and don't give them much direction, or only a few verbal pointers, they're left to improvise. And they cut so many people's hair on any given day that they're not going to try super hard to make it look great.

So, here's what to do:

1. Let your hair grow out until it's quite long. You want there to be a lot of hair to work with so you don't limit your options.

2. Find an expensive stylist in your area. Use Yelp to locate an expensive hair dresser in your area with a lot of good reviews.

3. Go to the stylist and tell them you're looking for a new style. Let them know if you want it to be more conservative or a bit on the edgier side. Discuss the options with them to let them know you really care

about the cut you're about to get – they'll try harder.

4. 95 percent of the time you're going to get a really nice haircut that complements your face shape and leaves you looking fresh as hell.

5. Take photos of your hair from the front, sides, and back.

6. Next time you need a cut, go to a regular barber and present him with these photos.

That's it. You eat the cost of an expensive haircut one time and then enjoy cheap imitations until you decide you want a new style. And, most importantly, you enjoy the boost in confidence that comes along with having a dope haircut.

20. How to Control Your Mental State in Times of Anxiety and Stress

In 2005, two professors at the University of California, Joanna Arch and Michelle Craske, performed a study on a group of undergraduate students (19). Their intention was to determine if a period of focused breathing would decrease the intensity of the students' negative emotional responses to a series of aversive images.

The students were split into two groups. One group was led through a period of 15 minutes of focused breathing while the other was led through a period of 15 minutes without any particular focus.

Before and after these 15 minutes, the students were exposed to a set of neutral slides. The focused breathing group maintained consistent, positive responses to the slides. The other group did not. After their 15 minute period that lacked a focus, the second group recorded significantly more negative responses to the neutral images.

After this, both groups were asked if they wanted to view negative, aversive images. The first group was far more willing to view these images. This fact combined with the different responses to the neutral images led Arch and Craske to the following conclusion:

"The lower-reported negative and overall affect in response to the final slide blocks, and greater willingness to view optional negative slides by the focused breathing group may be viewed as more adaptive responding to negative stimuli. The results are discussed as being consistent with emotional regulatory properties of mindfulness."

In other words, focused and mindful breathing leads to a greater ability to control and regulate your emotions. This shouldn't come as a shock to you. Focused breathing is the number one prescription of doctors to patients with severe anxiety, and it's a core function of how the mindfulness meditation we explored earlier works.

Hack 20: Focused Breathing

Focusing on your breathing calms your nerves. It forces you to pull your mind away from whatever is eating away at your tranquility and killing your confidence. When you're thinking about your breathing, you're likely to take deeper breaths that will lower your heart rate and your blood pressure. And it's very difficult to think or worry about anything else. For this reason, it's a hack that boosts short-term confidence.

Applying it is straightforward. Breathe in through your nose and deep into your belly. You should feel your belly button expand forward as you do this. After this, breathe out fully, again through your nose so that you feel your belly sink back in and towards your spine.

Do this and count at least ten breaths. Afterwards, you should feel a lot better.

I'll note that this may seem similar to the breath-based meditation covered earlier in the book, and it is. But I'll point out one major distinction: this is meant to be used in public situations when you need a spur-of-the-moment fix, whereas the aforementioned meditation is meant to be done in peace and quiet, for an extended period of time.

21. How to Speak Deeply with Confidence and Authority

Imagine that you're sitting on a bench and waiting at the doctor's office or waiting for the bus. Let's say waiting for the bus, to make this visualization a bit easier.

You notice a man walking towards you out of the corner of your eye. As you turn, you see that he's hunched over and looking at the ground. He's not particularly old, just seemingly weak and insecure. You look back ahead.

"Excuse me," calls out a deep voice from beside you.

What do you do?

Now let's take a step back and rewind. You're sitting at the same bus stop, all alone. Again you catch a person walking towards you out of the corner of your eye. This time you turn and see a tall man with wide shoulders strutting your way. You hold eye contact with him for a minute and then turn back to look ahead.

"Excuse me," calls out a voice from beside you.

This time it's not deep, but rather high pitched and frail, like that of an old women. How do you react?

Do you see what I'm getting at? Both of these situations seem odd because we instinctively link deep voices to characteristics like strength, confidence, and authority. Dwayne "The Rock" Johnson is a big dude and he speaks like one. Steve Jobs was an incredible innovator and marketer. No one will argue that. But watch his videos and listen to his voice. He sounds rather weak and insecure, nothing like The Rock.

Hack 21: Deep Belly Speaking

The difference between these people is how they speak. To speak in a deep, authoritative tone you must use your full diaphragm. This is known as speaking from your belly. Or speaking from your balls.

Men with deep voices do this, either naturally or because they've learned how. Men with shallow, weak voices do not. They instead speak from their chests or throats. Not only does this sound weaker, but the sound does not travel as far. That's why people like this are often asked to repeat themselves – something that will often damage your short-term confidence.

To internalize this concept I want you to perform the following exercise.

1. Take five breaths through your nose and deep into your belly, so that it rises and expands as you breathe. As you exhale, say "hello" each time.

2. Take five breaths through your mouth and into your chest, so that is rises and expands as you breathe. As you exhale, say "hello" each time.

3. Take five shallow breaths through your mouth and into your throat. As you exhale, say "hello" each time.

How do you sound each time? Do it again if you have to.

If you're doing it right, your voice should be rather deep for the belly breaths, high pitched for the throat breaths, and somewhere in between for the chest breaths.

Do it again and feel your belly, your chest, and your throat vibrate as you go. Make sure that you're speaking from your belly. This will reinforce the focused breathing from the last hack and change how you speak. People will perceive you as more confident and you'll embody this confidence as a result. And, of course, your short-term confidence will improve.

22. A Strange Trick to Shock Yourself and Reduce Your Inhibitions

It was a Friday night. The previous week I'd broken up with my girlfriend of almost a year. I hadn't spoken to another girl since then. I wasn't over her. But it was time to try and begin the moving on process.

I walked into a crowded nightclub with a good friend of mine and several of his buddies. This was a buddy that I used to go out with "on the prowl" with the intention of meeting new women. He was good. And so was I. But at that moment, I fully felt like I'd 'lost it.'

As my gaze centered on a cute brunette with long, curly hair and a slim figure, my stomach tightened up. I looked away. My friend noticed.

"You're not going to be a bitch all night," he said, in a tough-love sort of way.

I let the opportunity pass. And the next one. And the next one after that.

"Motherfucker," I muttered under my breath, "this

isn't going to happen." I reasoned that I'd have to push through the internal resistance and images of my ex in my mind at some point. But logic wasn't enough.

"I'm approaching her," I said to my buddy while motioning to a petite blonde at the bar, "and I'm going to be super direct. Don't let me back down."

He smiled at me and held eye contact. "There's no time like the present."

And so I walked straight over. "Hi," I shouted, "I just had to tell you that you're super fucking cute." She blushed and we chatted for a few minutes before I retreated back to my friend.

"All right. I feel awesome now; let's do this." The rest of the night, my inhibitions were lowered, and I proceeded to approach at least ten other women in the same manner.

Hack 22: The Bold Approach

While my above example took place in a nightclub, I've executed the same maneuver (albeit a bit toned down – swearing at a nightclub is more acceptable) in grocery stores, shopping malls, or just on the street. Usually it's with the intent of meeting new women. But the first approach has the same result every time: I feel insecure and anxious beforehand, but unstoppable and confident once I get myself to do it.

The second, third, and fourth approaches are always a breeze. I noticed this trend and began to approach often upon catching myself in down moods. The rush of the approach – and the rush of rejection (when it happens) – is like a hard drug: the effect is immediate and intense.

Use this hack whenever you need a boost of energy and confidence when you're in public – it's like a steroid for short-term confidence. After you approach a cute girl walking down the street, you feel as if your balls just grew to the size of bowling balls. I'd suggest doing it before a date or job interview to get loose, or just once a day to keep yourself honest.

All you do is go up to a cute girl (stop her if she's walking by saying "excuse me" in a deep, loud voice) and say, "I just had to tell you that you're looking adorable today." Whether or not you want to introduce yourself after this and continue the conversation is up to you.

23. The Secret to Dressing Sharply and Appearing Confident

"If you look good, you feel good. If you feel good, you play good. If you play good, they pay good."

This is a quote from the former NFL star of the Dallas Cowboys, Deion Sanders. And it's true.

How do you feel when you're wearing that new shirt that you know you look fresh in? Or how do you feel after getting that slick new haircut?

Conversely, how do you feel when you're wearing your pajamas out to the grocery store and you run into that cute girl from the gym? Or how do you feel when you get a haircut that's botched?

I think you get the point. We naturally feel more confident when we're looking fresh. And we oftentimes feel insecure when we know that we're not looking so hot.

Once you've built a solid long-term confidence this shouldn't hold true. You should still be able to feel confident even if you know that women might not find you as attractive as if you were looking great. It might not be an optimal time to approach that cutie, but it shouldn't make you insecure.

23. Excess Clothes Removal

The fact still remains that we tend to naturally feel a bit more confident if we're looking on point. We covered how to get a great haircut earlier, but here we'll deal with clothes. This hack is all about throwing away clothes that don't fit you.

Style is subjective. The only close to universal principle that holds true is that you should wear clothes that fit you. For men this means shirts that hug your chest and shoulders and don't fall far below your waist – not shirts that hang down to your knees like in 90's rap videos and also not shirts that stretch out at your chest so that your nipples are popping though. It also means pants that are relatively form fitting and aren't too long – not pants that squeeze your legs and expose your ankles like a punk rocker or pants that sag down on your ass and bunch up all over your shoes.

Try on all of your clothes, assess them by these factors in the mirror, and donate the clothes that don't fit. There's a bunch of charities that will swing by your house and pick up unwanted clothes and give them to people who can't afford them. Just Google "clothes donation [your city name]."

This will clean up some space in your home and

ensure that you're not wearing that ten year old football jersey that makes you look like a thug. Well, honestly, I have a few of those, but they usually don't leave the house.

All you need is a few outfits that fit for hitting up the gym, going to work, and going out. By making sure you always adhere to this principle, you'll boost your short-term confidence permanently.

24. A 5 Minute Activity That Will Relieve Depression and Invigorate You

Do you enjoy taking a nice warm shower?

I certainly do. I'll stay in there and relax for so long that my fingers get all weird and wrinkly. I always feel better after a long, warm shower.

What about cold showers? Do you enjoy those?

I can't stand them. I'll only take one if I find myself disgustingly dirty *and* I happen to be somewhere where the warm water isn't functioning... Until recently, at least.

That's because there's conclusive research that's found a couple of shocking benefits of taking cold showers. A 2008 study was conducted to test the hypothesis that cold showers could be used as a treatment for depression [20].

The evidence that supported this hypothesis is as follows:

"Exposure to cold is known to activate the sympathetic nervous system and increase the blood level of beta-endorphin and noradrenaline and to increase synaptic release of noradrenaline in the brain as well. Additionally, due to the high density of cold receptors in the skin, a cold shower is expected to send an overwhelming amount of electrical impulses from peripheral nerve endings to the brain, which could result in an anti-depressive effect."

In other words: exposing ourselves to cold temperatures activates the nervous system in a way that releases certain hormones and neurotransmitters that serve to combat the negative feelings of being depressed. And what did they find?

"Practical testing by a statistically insignificant number of people, who did not have sufficient symptoms to be diagnosed with depression, showed that the cold hydrotherapy can relieve depressive symptoms rather effectively."

Basically they weren't able to prove anything 100% conclusive, but they did find that the therapy worked in terms of relieving depressive symptoms. They just didn't conduct it on a large enough sample size of clinically depressed patients to qualify it as a medically accepted treatment option.

And this actually makes it all-the-more of a quality confidence hack. We aren't trying to defeat depression here. But we are trying to relieve depressive moods in order to get out of our heads and be more confident.

Hack 24: Cold Showers

The other main benefit cold showers will provide in regard to your confidence is a huge boost of energy. As soon as you step into a cold shower, you'll begin to breathe deeply – this is your body's natural response.

This deep breathing combined with the increased blood flow and general awakening effects you experience from a cold shower will invigorate you and prepare you to crush the rest of your day.

This is because we're inherently more confident when we're energized. When we're feeling tired or lethargic it's very hard to immerse yourself in the moment. This is why we tend to think negative, depressing thoughts at night, but gain a clear perspective on things in the morning when we're fresh.

For these reasons, cold showers boost your short-term confidence. I suggest taking one every morning, and later in the day if you need another boost of confidence and energy before departing your house.

I prefer to start out cold and then switch to warm water after two or three minutes, so that I'm not shivering when I exit the shower.

In terms of the temperature, set it about as cold as you can handle. Even if this isn't very cold at first, you'll still reap the benefits and your body will gradually adapt to colder water as you go.

How to Combine These Hacks and Create Powerful, Custom Confidence Stacks

Lately, the idea of 'habit stacks' has become extremely popular. A habit stack is effectively a routine of a handful of habits that can be completed together in a short period of time. The idea is that doing a series of related habits in quick progression will create a far more powerful effect than doing them alone in isolation. It also makes it easier and more practical to incorporate multiple new habits into your life.

This principle couldn't hold true anywhere more than with the confidence hacks I just shared with you. If you can find three to five hacks that resonate with your current situation and that can be done together, you will achieve an incredible boost in short-term confidence.

Below I'll offer you a few examples of 'confidence hack stacks' that I use.

Hack Stack 1: To be used in public, social situations

1. Deep, focused breathing (hack #20)

2. Conscious smiling (hack #6)

3. Powerful eye contact (hack #5)

4. Deep belly speaking (hack #21)

Hack Stack 2: To be used at home in isolation (e.g. when you wake up in the morning)

1. Count your blessings (hack #10)

2. Cold shower (hack #24)

3. I love myself affirmation (hack #3)

4. Power posing (hack #13)

Hack Stack 3: To be used before bed

1. Breath-based meditation (hack #2)

2. The daily review (hack #15)

3. Pre-bed mental exhaustion (hack #16)

4. The daily goal (for tomorrow – hack #18)

These are all **extremely** powerful routines. I honestly only use these confidence hacks in stacks at this point because it makes them that much more practical and effective. With that being said, create your own stacks using the hacks I've shared with you, and use them to create a stronger, more dominant, more confident presence and mindset.

Godspeed,

David

The Biggest Risk is Not Taking Action

The rules, habits, and techniques in this book are only effective if you actually put them to use.

That's why I created an online "bootcamp" course. This course will radically enhance your confidence, charisma, strength, and motivation in under a month.

It's a series of daily "missions" or challenges that will keep you accountable and force you to integrate a set of key habits, behaviors, and beliefs into your everyday life.

It's called 28 Days to Alpha:

I invite you to read more about the course by navigating to **www.28DaysToAlpha.com**.

Can You Do Me a Favor?

Thank you for buying and reading my book. I'm confident that you're well on your way to developing and refining your confidence level if you apply what's written inside.

Before you go, I have a small favor to ask. Would you take a minute to write a brief blurb about this book on Amazon? Reviews are the best way for independent authors (like me) to get noticed and sell more books. I also read every review and use the feedback to write future revisions – and future books, even.

Thank you.

My Other Books

If you enjoyed this book, you'll find my others awesome, too. They're all available on Amazon. Here are a couple of similar titles of mine:

1. *Dominate: Conquer your fears. Become the man you want to be.*

2. *Shredded Beast: Get lean. Build muscle. Be a man.*

3. *The Book of Alpha: 30 Rules I Followed to Radically Enhance My Confidence, Charisma, Productivity, Success, and Life*

About the Author

David De Las Morenas is an engineer, personal trainer, and internet entrepreneur known for his bestselling books on men's health.

You can follow him at: **www.HowToBeast.com**

Scientific References

1. Neurobiological Mechanisms of the Placebo Effect, Fabrizio Benedetti, Helen S. Mayberg, Tor D. Wager, Christian S. Stohler, and Jon-Kar Zubieta, The Journal of Neuroscience, 9 November 2005, 25(45)

2. Cooper, Douglas P., Jamie L. Goldenberg, and Jamie Arndt. "Empowering the self: Using the terror management health model to promote breast self-examination." Self and Identity 10.3 (2011): 315-325.

3. Martin, Chloé D., and Peter Salovey. "Death attitudes and self-reported health-relevant behaviors." Journal of health psychology 1.4 (1996): 441-453.

4. Vail, Kenneth E., et al. "When Death is Good for Life Considering the Positive Trajectories of Terror Management." Personality and Social Psychology Review 16.4 (2012): 303-329.

5. Blackie, Laura ER, and Philip J. Cozzolino. "Of Blood and Death A Test of Dual-Existential Systems in the Context of Prosocial Intentions." Psychological science 22.8 (2011): 998-1000.

6. Kilpatrick, Lisa A., et al. "Impact of mindfulness-based stress reduction training on intrinsic brain connectivity." Neuroimage 56.1 (2011): 290-298.

7. Aron, Arthur. "The Transcendental Meditation Program in the College Curriculum: A 4-Year Longitudinal Study of Effects on Cognitive and Affective Functioning." College Student Journal 15.2 (1981): 140-46.

8. Schimel, Jeff, et al. "Not all self-affirmations were created equal: The cognitive and social benefits of affirming the intrinsic (vs. extrinsic) self." Social Cognition 22.1: Special issue (2004): 75-99.

9. Paulhus, Delroy L. "Bypassing the will: The automatization of affirmations." Handbook of mental control (1993): 573-587.

10. Willis, Janine, and Alexander Todorov. "First impressions making up your mind after a 100-ms exposure to a face." Psychological science 17.7 (2006): 592-598.

11. Droney, Joylin M., and Charles I. Brooks. "Attributions of self-esteem as a function of duration of eye contact." The Journal of social psychology 133.5 (1993): 715-722.

12. Lau, Sing. "The effect of smiling on person perception." The Journal of Social Psychology 117.1 (1982): 63-67.

13. Frank, Mark G., and Paul Ekman. "PHYSIOLCGIC EFFECTS OF THE SMILE." (1996).

14. Ekeland, E., et al. "Can exercise improve self

esteem in children and young people? A systematic review of randomised controlled trials." *British journal of sports medicine* 39.11 (2005): 792.

15. Fox, Kenneth R. "The effects of exercise on self-perceptions and self-esteem." Physical activity and psychological well-being 13 (2000): 81-118.

16. Carney, Dana R., Amy JC Cuddy, and Andy J. Yap. "Power posing brief nonverbal displays affect neuroendocrine levels and risk tolerance." Psychological Science 21.10 (2010): 1363-1368.

17. Wood, Brittany, et al. "Light level and duration of exposure determine the impact of self-luminous tablets on melatonin suppression." Applied ergonomics 44.2 (2013): 237-240.

18. Spangler, Todd. "Netflix Remains King of Bandwidth Usage, While YouTube Declines." Variety.com. May 14 2014.

19. Arch, Joanna J., and Michelle G. Craske. "Mechanisms of mindfulness: Emotion regulation following a focused breathing induction." Behaviour research and therapy 44.12 (2006): 1849-1858.

20. Shevchuk, Nikolai A. "Adapted cold shower as a potential treatment for depression." Medical hypotheses 70.5 (2008): 995-1001.

Made in the USA
San Bernardino, CA
15 May 2020